MW00785089

Intelligent Analysis:

How to Defeat Uncertainty in High-Stakes Decisions

By Jay Grusin, PhD

with Steve Lindo

Intelligent Risk Management Publications

Endorsements

Intelligence Experts

"In the 20-plus years that I worked with Jay at CIA I knew him as both a highly regarded analyst and trainer of analysts. In this book, Jay combines that expertise with Steve's to give senior executives in the private sector a new and powerful approach to identifying and managing risks that can undermine corporate outcomes. At the same time, the book offers private-sector analysts a step-by-step approach to producing assessments that support near- and longer term strategic goals."
—**Michael Morell**, Former Acting and Deputy Director, CIA

"For over a decade at the Central Intelligence Agency, Jay Grusin and I worked on some of the toughest analytic challenges the Nation faced in Latin American and Asia. The techniques we used to manage risk, test assumptions, and deal with conflicting, incomplete, and sometimes inaccurate data—all presented in this readable book—are directly applicable to the business world. There is theory and then there is practice. Theory is cheap; the "how to" is priceless. This is the "how to."
—**Marty Petersen**, Former Deputy Executive Director of the CIA and Founder, Sherman Kent School of Intelligence Analysis

"There's a fine line between a disaster and a good story. The tools and techniques in *Intelligent Analysis* can help decisionmakers stay on the right side of that line."
—**Joe Gartin**, Former CIA Chief Learning Officer

Business Experts

"The analytical process described in Jay and Steve's book has been thoroughly field-tested in the intelligence space and adapted in a both creative and practical manner to the business context. Organizations who adopt these principles and methods are building a crucial competence for survival and success in today's uncertain times."
—**Leo M. Tilman**, Author of *Agility and Financial Darwinism* and Founder/CEO, Tilman & Company

"In this book, Jay and Steve lay out structured analytic techniques, which have been honed in the Intelligence Community, that can be used by business leaders to make better executive decisions, and by everyone to improve their personal choices."
—**Dr. Ray O. Johnson**, Former Senior Vice President and Chief Technology Officer, Lockheed Martin Corporation

"The collaboration of Steve and Jay merging disciplines from stringent CIA protocols with traditional business intelligence is remarkable and looks at data analysis and decision making through a new lens. This book provides detailed and actionable tools that will have an immediate impact on any business. An absolute must read for Senior Executives with the desire for objective, thorough, trusted data upon which they can make the best decisions."
—**Diane F. Adams**, Board Member and Former Chief Marketing and Innovation Officer

More Intelligence Experts

"Hats off to Steve Lindo and Jay Grusin for *Intelligent Analysis* – a no nonsense guide on assessing risk and building confidence in business decisions. With clear, straight-forward templates, the authors show how anyone can apply structured analytic techniques not only to improve their judgments, but also better explain the basis for those judgments. Whether you are considering a merger or acquisition, planning your next strategic investment, or forecasting future returns, Intelligent Analysis is a solid bet when it comes to strengthening your hand and bolstering your bottom line."

—**Mark Bellamah**, Former Senior CIA Officer, Founder and President, Black Lotus

"Jay and Steve have keenly navigated all of the noise surrounding big data to craft a targeted guide that arms executives and business analysts alike with the tools of rigorous analytic tradecraft to stress-test decisions. Their workbook is masterfully designed to both inform and teach readers through helpful exercises how to generate authoritative insights when, invariably, information gaps persist and unbiased inferences must be made."

—**Mary Majoros**, US Senior Intelligence Service Officer, Private industry executive

More Business Experts

"Simple, relevant steps to improve decision making are explored in the text. These should allow for improved decision making in my organization."

—**Howard Fields**, Senior Vice President, Investment Management Firm

"This book is a must read for any executive, management consultant, or business school professor seeking to improve high-stakes decision making. The authors hone techniques used by the intelligence community to minimize emotion and bias in decision making by setting up a framework that focuses on analytics."

—**Dennis Cuneo**, Senior Vice President (retired), Toyota

"The book masterfully brings forth the great interpolation between decision-making theory and the real business implications of decisions, which is crucial to any organization's long-term success. The exposition deftly combines the challenges faced by business leaders, the strategies employed by intelligence agencies, and practical examples that illustrate their use in business. The exposition deftly combines the challenges faced by business leaders, the strategies employed by intelligence agencies, and practical examples that illustrate their use in business."

—**Cristian Zarcu**, President/COO TradeDynamiX, Former Managing Director- Lazard, Wachovia Securities and Bank of America

"This book offers a remedy for one of the banking industry's weakest spots – risk management by prescription, which is completely inadequate for systemically uncertain situations such as pandemics. At times like these, it's vital that decisions be guided by clear goals, which Jay and Steve recognize in their chapter on the Key Intelligence Question. The discipline of making assumptions and questions explicit, followed by data-driven testing, can greatly improve the way bank risk managers support key decision-makers in their institutions."
—**Federico Galizia**, Chief Risk Officer, Interamerican Development Bank

"Adopting *Intelligent Analysis* will bolster the external credibility of M&A, divestitures, joint ventures, restructurings, and other transformative strategic actions. This is essential for companies that are assessed by financial firms that mainly focus on "what can go wrong."
—**Joel Lustig**, Former Head of Credit Ratings Advisory at Credit Suisse Investment Banking Former Senior Credit Officer at Moody's Investors Service

"*Intelligent Analysis* provides practical tools and proven techniques to produce objective, evidence-based analysis. It is a much needed "how to guide" for critical thinking to support decision making under uncertainty."
—**Roger Chen**, Head of Enterprise Risk Analytics and Reporting, New York Life

"This book provides an exceptional framework and tools, capable of defeating these threats and protecting the process, as well as its conclusions, in a robust methodology that can be executed consistently and delivered, as actionable intelligence, in a manner highly compatible with executive thinking. A must-read for risk management professionals intent on providing valuable insights that influence successful strategic decisions.
—**Bob Bowman**, Sr. Director, Risk Management, The Wendy's Company

"Organizations that struggle to establish a balanced decision-making process that is rigorous, agile, and collaborative, will find the disciplined and field-tested methods described in Jay's and Steve's book to be a powerful resource."
—**Angela Patel**, Enterprise Risk Management Program Leader, Amazon Web Services

Intelligent Analysis:
How to Defeat Uncertainty in High-Stakes Decisions

By Jay Grusin, PhD, with Stephen Lindo

Copyright © 2021 by
Jay Grusin, PhD , The Analytic Edge
Steve Lindo, SRL Advisory Services

No part of this book may be reproduced or used in any manner without the prior written permission of the copyright owner, except for the use of brief quotations in a book review.

Articles from *The Economist* are used with permission.

First Edition June 2021

ISBN: 978-1-7373019-0-5

Published in the United States by
Intelligent Risk Management Publications
6224 Cowell Road
Brighton, Michigan 48116
www.IntelligentRiskManagement.solutions

Edited by: Lois Maharg, On the Mark Editing

Book Design, Cover and Typesetting by
Cynthia J. Kwitchoff (CJKCREATIVE.COM)

Note to Readers

All statements of fact, opinion, or analysis expressed in this book are those of the authors and do not reflect the official positions or views of the Central Intelligence Agency (CIA) or any other US government agency. Nothing in the contents should be construed as asserting or implying US government authentication or information or CIA endorsement of the author's views. This material has been reviewed by the CIA to prevent disclosure of classified material.

ABOUT THE AUTHORS

Dr. Jay Grusin has served as an intelligence analyst and manager and teacher of analysts for over 40 years.

In 2008, he completed a 29-plus-year career at the Central Intelligence Agency, and since then has provided management and intelligence training across the private and public sectors.

Dr. Grusin is a member of the CIA's Senior Intelligence Service and received the Agency's Distinguished Career Intelligence Medal in recognition of his contributions, which include helping create and deliver an analytic training course that redefined how intelligence analysis would be taught at the CIA and led the development/delivery of the first sequenced management/ leadership curriculum.

Beginning in 2018, Dr. Grusin teamed with Steve Lindo to establish Intelligent Risk Management LLC. Together they developed and delivered a series of workshops, and now this book, for private sector clients based on how to apply these same tools and processes to help identify and manage risk and uncertainty.

Dr. Grusin earned his MA and PhD at the University of Arizona. He and his wife, Sarah, live outside of Ann Arbor, MI.

Steve Lindo is a financial risk manager with over 30 years' experience managing risks in banking, asset management and insurance.

He currently is a Lecturer and Course Designer in Columbia University's M.Sc. in Enterprise Risk Management program, as well Co-Principal of Intelligent Risk Management LLC, an executive education and advisory partnership which uses analytical methods pioneered by the US intelligence services to enhance decision-making by enterprises across all industries.

Mr. Lindo's earlier career includes executive positions with Fifth Third Bancorp, GMAC Financial Services (now Ally Financial), Cargill Financial Services, First National Bank of Chicago (now part of JPMorgan Chase) and Lloyds Bank, in the US, UK, Spain and Brazil.

In 2010, Mr. Lindo completed a two-year engagement as Executive Director of PRMIA – The Professional Risk Managers' International Association, a non-profit member organization with over 75,000 members in 198 countries.

Mr. Lindo is a regular presenter at conferences, webinar host and author of risk management articles and case studies.

He has a BA and MA from Oxford University and speaks fluent French, German, Spanish and Portuguese. He and his wife Marcie live near their grandchildren in Columbus, Ohio.

TABLE OF CONTENTS

ACKNOWLEDGMENTS

First, a separate thank-you to my life partner, Sarah Grusin. A former writer for the Smithsonian's National Museum of Natural History, she braved the first drafts that led to multiple rewrites and just made it better and more accessible to readers. Years of feedback and questions from hundreds of students from across the US intelligence services and law enforcement challenged my approach to teaching analysts and let me know what they needed—and didn't need—to be successful.

Outside reviewers from in and outside the US intelligence services made multiple useful comments on the substance. They were Frans Bax, David Cariens, Dan Luria, Marjorie Halpren, Ed Mickolus, and Neil O'Leary. With Bob Degross, my teaching partner at CIA for close to 10 years, I worked with hundreds of first-line managers of analysts who expanded our understanding of the challenges of collaborating across some 20 different US intelligence organizations. In addition, over the years during and after retirement, nuanced conversations with other colleagues steeped in the business of intelligence deepened my understanding of key concepts.

Special thanks to the directors of the Sherman Kent School for Intelligence Analysis at CIA that afforded me multiple opportunities. The same for my contractor program managers from Leidos, Chris Whitman, Lisa Wisner, Carol Parry, and John Soldner, who provided opportunities to support other analytic training programs. John Stolter, head of Analytic Advantage, opened still other doors for me. My neighbor on Winans Lake, Scott Page, a well-known expert on modeling and decision-making, introduced me to Steve Lindo. Our editor, Lois Maharg, raised the quality of the text and spotted lapses in clarity with her sharp eye all with just the right touch. Designer Cynthia Kwitchoff of CJK Creative brought our manuscript to life. Cindy showed remarkable patience and skill in helping us navigate the publication process end to end.

Of course, any mistakes are ours. In particular, CIA analysts, especially retired ones, never stop being analysts and will be hard-pressed to resist making comments and suggestions. We welcome them.

Jay Grusin: JRGrusin@gmail.com
Steve Lindo: Steve.Lindo@gmail.com

PREFACE BY STEVE LINDO

Certainty	Risk	Uncertainty

Every business decision lies somewhere along this spectrum.

My involvement in the project which led to this book began four decades ago, when, as an idealistic college graduate, I chose to become a banker in order to play a part in the grand business cycle which produces wealth and economic progress. After a while, however, that ideal dimmed as banking became more industrialized and impersonal, driven by production and performance metrics, repetition, regulation, and not a little greed.

In 1994 I took on a new challenge by redirecting my efforts towards risk management, seeking a way to tame volatility in corporate earnings by understanding, measuring, and mitigating expected and unexpected losses. Over time, risk professionals like me have learned to master the process of understanding, measuring, and mitigating outcomes which are predictable. But our profession hasn't made much progress in understanding, measuring, and mitigating uncertainty, in spite of the many lessons provided by persistent market crashes, crises, and contagions. The reasons for this are unclear. Is it lack of frequency? Lack of predictability? Lack of business imperatives or resources? Or cognitive biases and lack of executive self-awareness?

Most likely, it's a combination of all of these. However, fortunately for me, the elusive path to understanding, measuring, and mitigating uncertainty appeared, ironically, in an entirely unexpected way—by meeting Jay. Three years after that auspicious encounter, I'm excited to show you how Jay and I have melded the rigorous analytical methods which he has practiced and honed over four decades with the business knowledge, behavioral insights, and risk management techniques which I've acquired during the same time.

What we will show you in the following pages is that making good decisions involving high stakes and uncertainty requires a significantly different mindset from an organization's default decision-making process, which is typically dictated by culture, hierarchy, personalities, data, and haste. Instead, the methods we describe emphasize discipline, objectivity, diversity, reason, and transparency. Most importantly, these methods don't interfere with the way an organization makes its high-stakes decisions. Instead, they add a protective layer of analytics that either validates a good decision or exposes its flaws, which could lead to catastrophic consequences. Regardless of your organization's risk tolerance, our methods will show you where a high-stakes decision you have to make lies on the uncertainty spectrum and what, if any, actions you can take to nudge the needle to the left.

I hope that the time you spend reading our work brings you rich rewards in terms of confidence in, or rethinking of, future decisions that are crucial to your organization's long-term success. Jay and I welcome all feedback on our methods and their impact on the sustainability of your organization, as well as on the trajectory of your professional career. You'll find our contact information at the front of this book.

PREFACE BY JAY GRUSIN

Steve's preface makes clear the "why," of Intelligent Analysis. Now let me explain the "how."

This book is based on the same "analytic tradecraft," a term for the mechanics of producing assessments, that I used and then taught during in my nearly 30 years at the Central Intelligence Agency and beyond, to support the decisions of the US Government's most senior political and military leaders. For decades, analytic tradecraft has been embedded in the analysts' DNA in training from their first day on the job and then in learning throughout their careers. In the CIA's high-pressure, high-stakes environment, analytic tradecraft's rigor and discipline have been crucial to minimizing the impact of biases and emotions that affect even the best analysts.

Analysts who work through this book will certainly improve their skills and value-added to their organizations and learn about the responsibilities that come with the job. Equally important, woven into the book are the clearly understood core values which analysts must live by and that are essential to their work. Even the most diligent analysts will be failures unless they internalize and hold constant the same non-negotiable values that have defined my work and are shared by analysts across all branches of the US intelligence services. The most important are unshakeable integrity, objectivity, a commitment to telling truth to power, and a laser focus on providing the assessments that their audiences need in order to be successful. In addition, the best analysts are driven by an insatiable curiosity and a capacity for hard work and building expertise, and they are relentless in figuring out what's happening, why, and why it matters. They recognize and learn from mistakes. I did.

Before I met Steve, all this "why and how" was confined to my world and had found little or no resonance in his. Early on, my post-retirement private sector work had shown that analytic tradecraft should have been readily transferable, but I was unable to "crack the code" that would make the process resonate with private sector decision makers. When Steve and I connected through a mutual acquaintance, he immediately saw the potential but also understood the challenges. To reach his audience, he saw that we could integrate our worlds if we changed the vocabulary and frame of reference, using an approach that focused on the decision and not how it was reached. Intelligent Analysis is the product of that integration.

It has not always been an easy journey, but it has been a wonderful learning experience for both of us and, so far, we have not found anyone else who has managed this crossover with success. We started the melding with an article on Target's rapid rise and fall in Canada, that validated our approach and made our business case. From there it was conferences, roundtables and, finally, workshops which we developed and successfully delivered to private-sector groups. And now, here is the book. It is heavily experiential, with chapters that include detailed explanations, practice exercises and then applications to each analyst's organization's mission. What is practiced can be applied immediately, and over the longer term the book can serve as a desk reference.

As I wrote the book I saw it initially as a memoir of sorts. But, now that it's complete, what I want to memorialize is not the work that I did during my intelligence career—that's all classified—but rather what matters most to me and was woven into every course I developed and taught: the skills and hard lessons—sometimes really hard lessons — I have learned about how to do the work, how to produce actionable intelligence that supports decision-making. More importantly, I wanted to pass on how intelligence analysts must see themselves in their roles and the values they must hold dear as they do their work.

What has been harder to convey on paper is the passion and enthusiasm I have for analytic work, which remains undimmed. Not every day at the CIA was magical, but I loved the work and have loved doing it since I retired. It has been challenging, rewarding, and fun, yes, fun. And I hope that some of this energy seeps from these pages as well. Of course, any mistakes are mine. CIA analysts, including retired ones, never stop being analysts and are unlikely to resist making comments and suggestions. We also welcome them.

Definitions of Key Terms

A more detailed glossary is in Appendix B

AUDIENCE: executive, or executives, responsible for making or contributing to decisions with major organizational impact, OR analysts tasked with assessing the potential positive or negative outcomes of those decisions.

ACTIONABLE INTELLIGENCE: term used to describe targeted assessments that executive decision makers can act on to meet known requirements; applies to both private and public sector decision makers.

ANALYTIC TRADECRAFT: also known as tradecraft, a term used to describe a set of standardized tools and processes that analysts in the US intelligence services have used for decades to produce consistently objective, evidence-based assessments for a wide range of audiences.

BOTTOM LINE UP FRONT, OR B.L.U.F.: in Intelligent Analysis, a tightly formatted lead paragraph that provides audiences with actionable intelligence in a complete response to specific audience questions. Each sentence provides a key element of the response that includes an assessment of the event, the most likely outcome, and why it matters to the audience.

HIGH-STAKES DECISION: A complex decision whose outcome is likely to affect a broad range of stakeholders and substantially or crucially impact the organization's near and/or long-term success and sustainability.

INFERENCE: a conclusion based on facts known or assumed to be true at the time they are expressed, and which are subject to change. In this book, inferences are structured as A + B → C. A and B are facts as known and C is the implied inference or insight/conclusion that can be drawn. The arrow (→) is a stand-in for agreed-upon language which US intelligence services use as caveats that describe the estimated level of probability that C will occur (likely, unlikely, etc.).

KEY INTELLIGENCE QUESTION, OR KIQ: a question developed collaboratively between analysts and the audience that captures the primary goal of a specific proposal or initiative; it's crafted against a set of criteria and answered in the B.L.U.F.

STRUCTURED ANALYTIC TECHNIQUES, OR SATS: a suite of qualitative frameworks that rely on structured discussions to help analysts mitigate the adverse impact of their cognitive limitations—biases, emotions, and mindsets that work against objective analysis.

US INTELLIGENCE SERVICES: collective term used in the book to describe the US intelligence community, a group of 18 US government intelligence agencies and subordinate organizations that work separately and together to conduct intelligence activities supporting the foreign policy and national security of the United States. The Office of the Director of National Intelligence (ODNI) plays a coordinating role over the intelligence community and leads the presidential briefing team.

Certainty	Risk	Uncertainty

INTRODUCTION

Intelligent Analysis: Decision-Making When Stakes and Uncertainty Are High

In March 2003, US President George W. Bush decided to invade Iraq. In September 2008, Henry Paulson, Secretary of the US Treasury, Timothy Geithner, President of the Federal Reserve Bank of New York, and Ben Bernanke, Chairman of the Federal Reserve Board, decided not to bail out Lehman Brothers.

The high-stakes decisions which confront most organizations don't involve consequences of the magnitude of these two situations. But they do involve the same cocktail of incomplete and inconclusive data, conflicting opinions, cognitive biases, emotions, influence, and intense time pressure. As if these factors don't offer sufficient distraction from the calm, reasoned analysis demanded by high-stakes decisions, their rarity presents its own obstacle in the form of lack of a well-honed decision-making approach to identify and weigh all the facts, risks, and uncertainties in such extreme circumstances. This is the process we call Intelligent Analysis. In this book we describe and demonstrate its power and importance and teach you how to use it.

Organizations which are best able to transform complex information into actionable intelligence win every time. Intelligent Analysis helps organizations gain these critical insights with consistently objective, evidence-based assessments, proactively tailored to meet senior executives' requirements. The power of Intelligent Analysis lies in the combination of senior executives who, when faced with high stakes and uncertainty, ask the question "**What am I missing?**"

and their decision support team being able to use Intelligent Analysis to an-swer that question.

One of our approach's most important features is that we gauge risk and uncertainty along a spectrum. At one end is certainty, where facts are incon-trovertible, and action is self-evident. The middle of the spectrum is occupied by risk, where possible outcomes, good and bad, are more or less understood and probabilities can be assigned and measured, vulnerabilities mitigated, and opportunities exploited. At the other end of the spectrum are uncertain envi-ronments where information gaps and unknowns generate multiple possible outcomes which significantly raise the odds of failure. Intelligent Analysis iden-tifies the point where the dividing line between risk and uncertainty is blurred or ignored, under the combined weight of tight time constraints, pressure to come to closure, emotions, biases, or just bad process. Where our approach is most valuable to senior executives is that it tests where any high-stakes deci-sion lies on this spectrum, regardless of how it was made. Specifically, it:

- "Debiases" decision-making by reducing the impact of mind-sets, emotions, models, algorithms, predictive analytics, or the loudest or most senior voice in the room.

- Brings consistency to decision-making by following the same path every time. Its discipline helps drive variations out of how decisions are made, which can change markedly among an organization's business units and functions, sometimes from meeting to meeting. It also makes how the decision was reached more transparent, defensible, and repeatable. Stake-holders can more easily understand the message, follow the argument, and know what to expect from each recommenda-tion.

- Leverages expertise and diverse thinking by encouraging col-laboration, creating an environment that leverages diverse views and expertise and integrates contributions from multi-ple players who often come to the table with competing agen-das, loud voices, and set opinions. Our approach also mitigates what is known as organizational silence, which occurs when participants in a discussion choose to remain on the sidelines rather than risk criticism or retaliation for speaking out (Morrison and Milliken, 2000). New or less experienced employees are especially prone to this behavior. The answer is always in the room and can come from the least expected source.

In the intelligence world, volatile, uncertain, and high-stakes situations occur 24/7. Terrorism, war, cyberattacks, drug cartels—these are just some of the volatile and uncertain situations which daily confront the US intelligence services who, over the course of the last 25 years, have developed and implemented a suite of analytical methods specifically designed to produce rigorous, objective, and transparent assessment of complex, high-stakes situations. Their applicability to the business world is demonstrated in figure 1, which shows how the two worlds match up.

The article on Target's disastrous foray into Canada, which is included as Appendix E in this book, provides a well-crafted business case that validates our collaboration. From this article we developed a series of successful workshops that we created and delivered and which refined our approach.

What's in Common	Intelligence Analysts	Private/ Nonprofit Sectors
Complex variables, high stakes	X	X
High degree of uncertainty and risk	X	X
Demanding decision makers	X	X
Conflicting information	X	X
Data saturation	X	X
Seniors with multiple information sources	X	X
Must manage public perceptions	X	X
Use of qualitative, quantitative tools	X	X

Figure 1. These two worlds share the same challenges in making high-stakes decisions.

This Book Is Structured to Reach Two Audiences

One of our challenges is introducing Intelligent Analysis to two very different audiences. For senior executives, this book focuses on explaining the "why"—the business case for why the more decision-making pressure they

Intelligent Analysis vs. Intelligence Analysis

Intelligent Analysis and Intelligence Analysis are substantively the same, but adopting a different label is not just a matter of semantics. While the US intelligence services and private sector share the same challenges, the tools and techniques which intelligence analysts use have found little or no traction outside that domain. This book uses Intelligent Analysis to signal a change in the narrative, incorporating important changes in how some of the concepts are framed, explained, and applied in exercises, while keeping the process intact.

face, the more they need Intelligent Analysis. For the analysts who support their organizations, however, this book provides a step-by-step guide to learning the mechanics of Intelligent Analysis—the "how" that drives how the results of Intelligent Analysis are delivered the same way every time, based on the US intelligence services' best tradecraft practices.

For Senior Executives

The table of contents provides a sense of the overall flow of the intelligent analytic process end to end. A summary page at the start of each chapter describes the basic concepts, practices, and methods that, together, give a good sense of the "connective tissue" that binds the parts together into a well-crafted analysis and recommendations. The rest of the chapter takes analysts through each step of the process.

The book is heavily experiential, with over 20 exercises included throughout the book. Each chapter starts with a detailed explanation, then the review of an example. In one long segment, the book uses a scenario where the executives of a large commercial real estate company have to decide whether or not to enter a new market, as a means to illustrate how Intelligent Analysis can be applied to decision-making.

Chapters end with the direct application of the lesson learned to a real-life project which each analyst brings to the exercises, ideally one which is work-related. To facilitate learning, each concept is framed in a matrix that requires analysts to become more deliberate about how they develop their assessments.

Figure 2 on the next page illustrates the overall course flow. Key terms are explained in the Key Definitions section up front as well as in an expanded Glossary in the Appendices. Source citations are shortened in the text, but a complete list follows the Glossary in the Appendices.

Think Like an Analyst, Become an Analyst, Add Value

"Analysts should be self-conscious about their reasoning processes. They should think about how they make judgments and reach conclusions, not just about the judgments and conclusions themselves. Thinking analytically is a skill like carpentry or driving a car. It can be taught, it can be learned, and it can improve with practice."

—Richards J. Heuer, *Psychology of Intelligence Analysis*

For Analysts

You will be taken on a deep dive beyond the chapter summaries and practice the takeaways from each chapter in a project selected from your own work.

Intelligent Analysis builds skills, improves your support for senior executives, and increases your organizational impact. This book gives you the tools and techniques that will enable you to consistently convey clear, evidence-based, actionable intelligence that meets your audience's requirements the same way every time right from *the first paragraph*, which we call the Bottom Line Up Front, or B.L.U.F. The heart of the skills acquired in order to perform Intelligent Analysis to the highest standard all come together in that carefully thought-out lead paragraph. It's the hard work that has to be done before the first word of the analysis is written down, which yields the rewards of increased impact and value added to the organization, and the potential to earn a seat at the table as decisions are made.

Specifically, each sentence in that first paragraph delivers part of the message in a fixed sequence that answers the decision-maker's specific requirements. The B.L.U.F. takes your audience from what's known about an event or development of interest to what's ahead and the implications for the organization—from the "what" to the "so what." Below is a more detailed breakdown of the B.L.U.F.'s seven components, each of which is covered in depth in this book.

Flow of Intelligent Analysis

Structured Analytic Techniques Shape Intelligent Analysis

Good Intelligence and Good Analysts Meet High Standards

Tailor Analysis to the Target Audience

Bottom Line Up Front Leads Assessment, Delivers Actionable Intelligence

Decision Maker Knowledge and Collaboration Shape Key Intelligence Question

Evidence-Based Decisions Mean First Collect, Count, and Array Data

Arrayed Data Answers Key Intelligence Question Through Inferences

A Deeper Look at Assumptions and Data Quality Sharpen Probability Estimates

Key Assumptions Check Tests Assumptions, Validates Proability Estimate and Data Reliability

Key Assumptions Check Results Estimate Most Likely Outcome, Implications, and Mitigation Strategies

A Clear Title, Drafting, and Summary Increase Impact

Figure 2. The flow of Intelligent Analysis is an end-to-end process.

Moving Your Audience from What's Known . . .
1. *What?* What development or event has prompted the question?
2. *Why now?* What is precipitating the event or development?
3. *How does it work?* Is there a process or terminology to be explained?
4. *What's the impact so far?* What has happened because of the event?

. . .To What's Next:
5. *What's ahead?* What's the "so what" for the audience?
6. *What are the implications?* What's "the so what of the so what" that explains the importance of what's ahead?
7. *What can be done to mitigate risks and exploit opportunities?*

The first four elements are reporting an event or development, which is the "what." It is aggregating data which can be useful for creating summaries or chronologies. The heart of Intelligent Analysis, however, is in the B.L.U.F.'s last three elements, where it is transformed into the "so what" and why it matters.

This book was developed to show analysts how to move from creating lists to producing analytic assessments that support decision-making and the organization's mission more broadly. It explains in detail how to craft each of these seven statements based on analytic tradecraft's best practices.

The book is formatted as a workbook that will both help you now and serve as a reference tool over the longer term as the tools and processes become more familiar. It's heavily experiential and focuses on your own work by including a short exercise at the end of each chapter which applies to your chosen project.

Each chapter includes a detailed explanation of how it fits into the intelligent analytic process, a blank template that requires you to think about the step more deliberately, at least one filled-in example template, a practice exercise, and finally an opportunity to apply the concept to the project which you selected from your own work. The process is sequential and needs to be done in order—no skipping or sliding through the work. Lessons learned can be applied immediately. A complete set of the book's templates is available in Microsoft Word form free of charge to every purchaser of the book.

Frequently Asked Questions Answered

Can I Use these methods alone in my place of work?

The short answer is yes, but our approach is best used in a small group or at least with one other person. Doing it solo makes it more challenging to stay focused and there is no one to check your work. Our blank templates and examples help mitigate these downsides because they serve as models and as checks on your work. This book is designed to serve as an ongoing reference tool. The first time through is just that—a start. As you work through the book, the various frameworks are formatted as tables that can be reproduced on your computer for later use.

Alternatively, a complete set of the book's templates in MS Word is available free of charge to every purchaser of the book by sending an email request to: **Intelligent.Analysis.2021@gmail.com**.

Can Intelligent Analysis also support personal decision-making?

As you work through the book, the application of Intelligent Analysis to life outside work becomes readily apparent, because it offers a more objective approach than the standard "pro and con" model, which always ends with the answer you want. It can be used on your own but is best shared with others who can help keep you honest. Some personal areas where our approach can be helpful include:
- Relocation
- Job change
- New home purchase
- Selecting a college
- Serving on committees or boards of civic and religious organizations

Last Reminders

Intelligent Analysis works for both senior executives and analysts across organizations and industries. Long experience in intelligence analysis, however, has shown that skipping steps or setting the process aside in favor of the loudest voice, a higher authority, or perceived time pressure can have serious adverse consequences. Moreover, this book's end-to-end approach provides a critical framework for analysts and facilitates the workflow.

- First and most importantly, this book provides a roadmap to make sure that analysis is thorough and there are no skipped steps. Senior executives trust that you have done the work, and anything short of completeness can mislead them, with potentially serious consequences to the organization.

- Second, knowing the target audience and what they need determines which data is selected from the deluge of reports, statistics, and other information available from multiple different data sources, narrowing the initial fire hose of information into a more manageable soda straw.

- Third, a set process helps mitigate "stuck-ness." Analysts often cite the inability to know where and how to start as their major analytic challenge. Knowing your audience, understanding their requirements, and developing the right Key Intelligence Question (KIQ) gives you that crucial starting point.

One last note. This book does not include any "correct answers." Instead, provided you study the frameworks and examples carefully and mimic them as you do the exercises, you will do fine. A chess analogy is useful when thinking about Intelligent Analysis: it's easy to learn the basics quickly, but it takes a lifetime of hard work to master. Our approach asks your brain to think differently and rearrange neurons that have shaped how you have learned to do your work. Some good advice is:

- Be patient with yourself.

- Trust the process and do the hard thinking up front.

- Don't cut corners; skipping steps comes to no good.

- Practice as often as you can and use this book as a reference tool.

- Have fun.

Intelligent Analysis is not a magic bullet. Getting to the B.L.U.F. is hard work, really hard work that stretches your critical thinking skills. However, it's a proven and potentially powerful path to improved critical thinking skills and the mindset required to consistently produce objective, evidence-based analysis which provides the best support to decision-makers.

Now Choose the Project That You Will Develop as You Work Through the Book

Answer the questions below. Understand that your project may become more focused or change significantly as you work through the exercises. So, don't worry about it.

Who is your audience?

_____

_____

_____

What is your project?

_____

_____

_____

Why does it matter?

_____

_____

_____

CHAPTER ONE

Structured Analytic Techniques Manage Biases, Gauge Risk and Uncertainty, and Foster Collaboration

"Weaknesses and biases inherent in human thinking processes . . . can be alleviated by conscious application of tools and techniques. Structured Analytic Techniques are the process by which collaboration becomes most effective."

—Richards J. Heuer, *Psychology of Intelligence Analysis*

SUMMARY

Main Points

- Structured Analytic Techniques (SATs) are a suite of qualitative frameworks that rely on structured discussions to help the audience mitigate the adverse impact of their cognitive limitations—biases, emotions, and mindsets—that undermine objective decision-making. We are born with biases and cannot disown them even when we try.

- The US intelligence services have used SATs for decades, especially for challenging issues when sharp differences and strong personalities impact objectivity.

- SATs test assumptions underpinning decisions, estimate probabilities, and identify strategies to mitigate risk or exploit opportunities. The discussions required foster collaboration across components.

Key Takeaways

Think of SATs as warning tools. While they are important in risk management, they are most valuable in uncertain decision-making environments when information gaps and multiple possible outcomes can undermine objective assessments in high-stakes situations.

Well over 80 SATs have been developed. This book uses two SAT frameworks:

- *The Key Assumptions Check (KAC)* tests the soundness of the assumptions that underpin the answer to the Key Intelligence Question (KIQ) (see chapter 5), including the estimated probability that the event or development will occur.

- *Indicators of change* gauge the impact of mitigation strategies.

Because other chapters go into much more depth on using these frameworks, this chapter's exercise focuses on their value in fostering collaboration and keeping the focus of discussions on the data, not on personalities. Specifically, the audience selects a collaboration challenge they are facing or expect to face and explains which tools might help them manage it.

CHAPTER 1:
Structured Analytic Techniques Manage Biases, Gauge Risk and Uncertainty, Foster Collaboration

"Weaknesses and biases inherent in human thinking processes . . can be alleviated by conscious application of tools and techniques. Structured Analytic Techniques are the process by which collaboration becomes most effective."
—**Richards J. Heuer,** *Psychology of Intelligence Analysis*

Goal: To understand that Structured Analytic Techniques (SATs) play multiple roles in Intelligent Analysis, including mitigating the impact of biases and emotions on objective analysis, testing the soundness of assumptions that underpin assessments, and fostering collaboration.

Objectives

At the end of this chapter, analysts will be better able to:

- Explain the development of SATs.

- Describe the biases that impact analytic objectivity and can derail decision-making and decision meetings.

- Apply SATs to a specific collaboration challenge they are facing.

Note: Understanding the utility of SATs is key to testing assessments, especially when making decisions in high-risk and uncertain operating environments. To deepen your understanding of SATs ahead of working through this chapter, we highly recommend that you read or review *A Tradecraft Primer: Structured Analytic Techniques for Improving Intelligence Analysis*, published online by the US government in 2009. Heuer's first four chapters are also fundamental to maximizing what you can take away from this brief introduction to SATs.

In high-risk environments, and even more so in uncertain decision-making environments, SATs can blunt the impact of your biases and emotions that get in the way of analytic objectivity. SATs are qualitative, that is, based on structured discussions. SATs bring rigor and discipline to an often ragged and unpredictable decision-making process; colleagues have referred to SATs as key in breaking up "log jams." The intelligence services can't afford to delay making assessments or settle for compromises forced by the loudest voice or press of time.

A Warm-Up Exercise: Let's Start with a Puzzle

Look at figure 3 and see if you can see what there is to be seen. The answer is on the last page of the chapter.

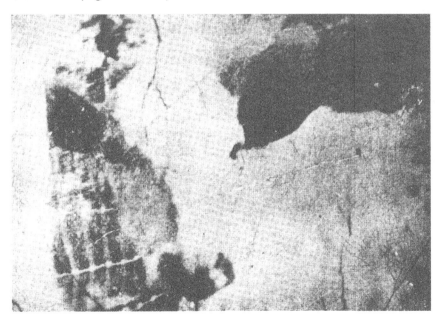

Figure 3. Can you see what there is to be seen?

Hard to See? The Cause Is in Your Head . . And Stuck There

Imagine the picture is a stand-in for the data collected to answer the question, especially estimating probability. You are in a meeting where everyone has the same data, but stakeholders all see it differently. What's up with everyone? Richards Heuer in his seminal work, *Psychology of Intelligence Analysis*, asks the same question: "Why can't we see what there is to be seen [in the data]?" In his book Heuer argues that missing the picture—and arguments ensuing over the same data—is not our fault but rather comes from the worldview baked into our brains as we have grown into adults. And we are pretty much stuck with it.

Heuer asserts that what is in our heads undermines our ability to remain objective in the face of uncertainty. The US intelligence services have used SATs for over 30 years, and training in SATs has been mandated for all intelligence analysts in the US government since the 11 September attacks. At that time, US congressional and other investigators' postmortems determined that analysts failed to "connect the dots" and to question their own assumptions about sources and other possible outcomes." Figure 4 explains the most common biases that pose the most serious risks to objective analysis. They are drawn from the tradecraft primer on SATs but based on Heuer's work.

PERCEPTUAL BIASES	BIASES IN EVALUATING EVIDENCE
• **Expectations**. We tend to perceive what we expect to perceive. • **Resistance**. Perceptions resist change even in the face of new evidence. • **Ambiguities**. Initial exposure to ambiguous or blurred stimuli interferes with accurate perception, even after more and better information becomes available.	• **Consistency**. Conclusions from a small body of consistent data engender more confidence than those drawn from a larger body of less consistent data. • **Missing Information.** It is difficult to judge the potential impact of missing evidence, even if the information gap is known. • **Discredited Evidence**. Even evidence proven wrong may not be sufficient to change perceptions quickly.
BIASES IN ESTIMATING PROBABILITIES	**BIASES IN PERCEIVING CAUSALITY**
• **Availability**. Probability estimates are influenced by how easily we can image or recall similar instances. • **Anchoring**. Probability estimates are adjusted only incrementally. • **Overconfidence**. In determining levels of certainty, we are often overconfident, especially experts.	• **Rationality**. Randomness, accident and error tend to be rejected as explanations for observed events. • **Attribution**. Behavior of others is attributed to some fixed nature of the person or country, while our own behavior is attributed to the situation in which we find ourselves.

Figure 4. Biases that most impact objective analysis
(US Government, *A Tradecraft Primer*, 2009).

Not specifically named here is confirmation bias, where we tend to look for information that confirms our assumptions. This bias is especially damaging because it leads analysts consciously or unconsciously to select information that confirms their closely held views.

More Detail on Two Key Resources

Richards Heuer was part of the CIA's Directorate of Operations, which collects intelligence that analysts transform into actionable intelligence. Heuer transferred to the Directorate of Intelligence, which houses the analysts, where he turned to social science methodology to pursue a question of cognition: how we know what we know.

In chapter 2, Heuer draws on his 1980 article entitled "Perception: Why Can't We See What Is There to Be Seen." Here, he addresses the central question of why analysts fall short in reaching objective judgments. Heuer posits that the challenge is found in how the brain naturally falls back on inherent biases to deal with uncertainty. Biases are important, Heuer argues, for sorting through large volumes of data, but they can also be an analyst's worst enemy. In this regard, Heuer observed that even if we are aware of our biases, we are poorly equipped to counter them when faced with uncertainty. Tools and techniques that push us toward more critical thinking, such as structured discussions, can reduce the likelihood of poor decisions.

SATs Create a Process, Improve Outcomes

SATs properly employed are central to the success of Intelligent Analysis and at the heart of this book. The rigor and discipline they bring to the decision-making process can be the difference between an initiative's success and failure. When intelligence assessments don't hold up, more often than not they are process failures—not failures of intellect or expertise. Postmortems have shown that, in many instances, the analysts didn't use available tools or skipped or glossed over the steps developed and validated for years among the US intelligence services to protect them against jumping to conclusions or failing to adequately test assumptions. Of course, the same can be said for decision-making in the private and nonprofit sectors. The landscape is littered with failed mergers and acquisitions and culture clashes that did not end well. SATs are no guarantee of success, but as Heuer asserts, they help in managing biases and reduce the likelihood of error.

SATs:

- *Slow everyone down.* Structured discussions can push the group to be more deliberate and conscious about how they arrive at their assessment. For example, SATs block jumping to an answer.

- *Encourage evidence-based assessments.* SATs expose unstated assumptions and groupthink that can derail evidence-based discussions and discourage dissent. Decisions based on instinct or "gut feelings" may well be valid, but a few hours to stress test such assessments can validate them.

- *Foster collaboration.* The loudest or most senior voices or those claiming the most experience can shut down or discourage participation from those who are reluctant to dissent. SATs give team leaders tools to manage disruptors, ensure that everyone has a voice, more effectively leverage expertise and integrate multiple viewpoints.

- *Strengthen the assessment's credibility.* The results of an SAT exercise can be the basis for more clearly presented written or oral findings, especially in high-stakes decisions. Stakeholders who are skeptical of the process or dug into their positions can at least see a transparent, defensible argument and inclusive process.

Three Rules Key to Follow in Order to Make SATs Work

■ Accept SATs as validated tools to help identify/manage risk, not a box-checking exercise.

■ Obtain buy-in from participants: use a facilitator, trust the process, outlaw disruptors, set aside egos.

■ Ensure that senior management supports the process:

   ■ It is not cosmetic

   ■ Findings are taken seriously: ask questions, examine data critically

   ■ Be willing to change.

SATs can also mitigate three barriers that have long impacted both executive decision-makers and analysts.

Organizational silence: This is most common in meetings where participants or managers dominate the discussion. Others for multiple reasons choose to remain on the sidelines rather than risk criticism or retaliation for speaking out. New or less experienced staff are especially vulnerable. These are missed opportunities to solve tough problems. Consequences can be serious (Morrison and Milliken, 2000). The answer is always in the room and can come from unexpected sources.

Practical drift: Scott Snook first used the term practical drift in his book, *Friendly Fire* (Snook, 2000), to refer to avoidable systemic failures that contributed to the accidental downing of two US military helicopters by US forces in April 1994. Snook defines practical drift as the slow uncoupling of practice from written procedure. It occurs when agreed-upon procedures are sidestepped because they are perceived to be obstacles to getting the job done. Applied to Intelligent Analysis, it means skipping or glossing over required steps in the analytic process. This habit can quickly become the norm because "so far nothing has happened." The consequences of sloppy tradecraft have been serious and invariably cited as a cause of so-called intelligence failures.

Probability drift: A concept borrowed from mathematics; it negatively affects the internal alignment of an intelligence assessment. Specifically, it impacts assessments of the estimated level of probability that an event or development will occur. It surfaces when the estimates within an intelligence assessment change, from "probably" to "highly likely," for example, either because the analyst changed their mind or new information arrived and was integrated without accounting for the change in the rest of the document. It also happens in the review process when the document is edited without looking at the assessment as a whole. As a result, the audience is left without a net assessment and must guess the analyst's intent. There are no easy fixes. Every change requires a complete review of the assessment for alignment.

Facilitators in SAT Discussions Manage Process, Protect Equities

Facilitators are neutral and familiar with the SAT process. Their participation allows the group to focus on the issue rather than manage themselves and the process. Ahead of the meeting, facilitators can plan the agenda, including goals and ground rules, and provide materials to make sure participants understand the SATs that will be used. During the meeting, the facilitator initiates the discussion, keeps the group focused on the issue, and makes sure all voices are heard. Facilitators can also manage the inevitable disruptors. The US intelligence services have used them for years to good effect. We will see how the facilitator leverages SATs to solve a tough problem and encourage collaboration in a scenario that starts in chapter 9.

SATs Prompt Rethinking in Three Key Areas

The CIA's tradecraft primer on SATs divides the most widely used techniques into three groups (US Government 2009). The list given below is for reference. Turn to the primer for detailed discussions of each of the techniques. Note that while they are categorized, the techniques frequently overlap, and each can serve in multiple situations.

- *Diagnostic SATs push for transparency.*
    - Key Assumptions Check (KAC)
    - Quality of Information Check (level of confidence test)
    - Indicators/Signposts of Change

- *Contrarian SATs challenge current thinking.*
  - Devil's Advocacy
  - Team A/Team B
  - High-Impact/Low Probability
- *Imaginative Thinking SATs develop perspectives, alternatives.*
  - Structured Brainstorming
  - Red Team

The list of SATs developed over the years goes well beyond this short list, but these SATs are those used most frequently by the US intelligence services. This book draws exclusively on the three diagnostic tools that are of most practical use. They are especially effective in developing the B.L.U.F.'s last three elements that shift the story from what's known to what's ahead: include the most likely outcome, the level of estimated probability, and indicators of change that measure the effectiveness of mitigation strategies. The book also makes use of other frameworks developed specifically for the book and another one drawn from the Sherman Kent School.

Another Important Tool: Premortems Look Back to Look Forward

The book does not include the premortem SAT, but it's another important SAT to help groups avoid bad outcomes. Most readers have at least heard the term *postmortem*, which refers to looking back on an event to determine what went wrong and why. In a well-run postmortem, the team can usually sort out what went well and systemic shortfalls. Because they are looking backward, however, there is a tendency to look for blame and send participants into a defensive posture. These behaviors can sideline quiet or less senior participants who may have useful insights to add; the answer is always in the room. That said, what often surfaces in postmortems are problems that, if known and addressed ahead of time, could have altered the outcome. In 2007, Gary Klein, in *Harvard Business Review* (Klein, 2007), posited that an assessment done before the launch of a product or decision making process could also uncover these same vulnerabilities to improve the chances for success. We look ahead by looking backward. Nobel laureate Daniel Kahneman, in a 2014 video on YouTube (Premortem, 2014), explained premortems something like this:

Before the launch of a product, imagine a year down the road that an event derails the product. Write the history of that disaster. Figure 5 illustrates the difference between postmortems and premortems.

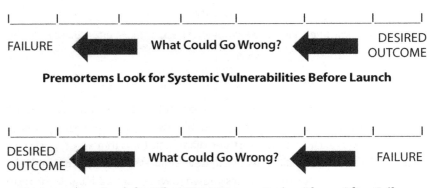

Figure 5. Premortems are proactive; postmortems look for blame.

In his YouTube video, Kahneman goes further, asserting that premortems are the only effective way to look ahead, because of the structured focus only on what *could* go wrong, *not* who did it. One of his most important points is that a properly run premortem encourages dissent and wide participation in a risk-free environment. To this end, premortems have been widely adopted across disciplines and business areas. For example:

- In the military they are used to plan operations.

- Hospitals have used premortem checklists that have led to major reductions in the spread of infection and improvements in surgery procedures.

- The walk around the aircraft that the captain makes during crew changes is also consistent with the premortem. These checks are not perfunctory; how many times have you been delayed because they found something?

- In France, premortems assumed there would be a fire in Notre Dame cathedral, and preplanning and twice-yearly practices prepared first responders to head for the most valuable objects for rescue.

Now It's Your turn

The book makes heavy use of SATs as diagnostic tools, but the exercise here focuses on their value in fostering collaboration. The exercise provides a template that can help you plan how to use SATs to manage a collaboration challenge that is work-related and involves at least two other colleagues. The exercise includes questions about which SAT you would find useful in managing your project. You may not be able to answer that now but think about it and refer to the primer.

EXERCISE:
Meet Your Own Collaboration Challenge

Instructions: Turn back to the SAT's listed above or, better still, to the primer and review the SATs. Think about which SAT(s) would help you manage your challenge more effectively. Note the explanations for when and how they are used and then the examples.

1. **Detail the issue: What is the collaboration challenge?** The challenge can be at work or in your personal life, club, or organization you work with or lead.

_____

_____

_____

2. **What is blocking collaboration? Here, point out the specific issue.** For example, is it peers, another component or group, or just sharp differences of opinion?

_____

_____

_____

3. **What SATs) might prove most useful?** Consult the SATs listed above or the primer for reference. More than one may prove useful. Explain the choice. Note: You may have to come back to this but see if you can identify an approach that would be helpful.

_____

_____

_____

4. **Who needs to be at the table to solve this problem?** Be specific. All stakeholders need to be part of the process. This can be other stakeholders at work
or in your organization.

---

5. **Would any outside experts be helpful?** What expertise might be missing
or would add another perspective?

Puzzle answer: It's a cow's head.

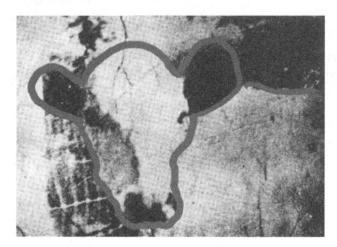

CHAPTER TWO

What Makes for Good Intelligent Analysis and Good Analysts

> "Learn your craft. And don't ever let a piece of writing out of your hands until it's as good as you can make it."
>
> —**Dan Jenkins**, Sportswriter, Author

Summary

Main Points

- The purpose of *Intelligent Analysis* is to provide audiences with actionable intelligence in assessments that convey a clear message.

- This book adheres to the US intelligence services' quality standards and production process. Both are immutable. Skipping or glossing over steps in the process will result in an assessment that fails to meet its audience's needs

- Intelligence analysts face multiple challenges, but the most successful show an insatiable curiosity, a capacity for work, and attention to detail, and they know their audience and understand their organization's mission.

Key Takeaways

The chapter provides important context for the rest of the book. It explains analysts' role in the intelligence cycle. The cycle flows in a loop that begins with requirements, collection of data in response to the requirements, analysis, and production, which in turn generates questions and new requirements.

The book defines the qualities of good Intelligent Analysis, and the methods used in this book map to the table. Chief among them are:

- Objectivity is non-negotiable.

- The audience's agenda drives everything.

- The argument is persuasive and easy to track.

- Visuals—graphics, charts, and tables—reinforce the main point and enhance impact.

- These qualities are reflected in a table that visualizes the US intelligence services' quality standards. The most critical qualities apply to developing a clear message that conveys actionable intelligence in the first paragraph.

The chapter's exercise requires analysts to assess a short article's (poor) clarity of message and then craft a lead sentence and summary that better capture it. Going over the qualities of good analysts begins to focus them on considering their roles.

CHAPTER 2:
What Makes for Good Intelligent Analysis and Good Analysts

"Learn your craft. And don't ever let a piece of writing out of your hands until it's as good as you can make it."

—**Dan Jenkins,** Sportswriter, Author

Goal: To provide an overview of the intelligent analytic process, explain the characteristics of good Intelligence and good analysts, and follow a deliberate and conscious process.

Objectives

At the end of this chapter, analysts will be better able to:

- Explain the flow of the Intelligent Analysis process and why actionable intelligence must be traceable, defensible, and repeatable.

- Articulate how US intelligence service standards of analytic quality define Intelligent Analysis.

- Describe the qualities common to good analysts.

- Apply what you have learned to assess a short article against analytic quality standards.

Defined Process Generates Actionable Intelligence

And so the hard work begins.

A former senior CIA officer and good friend has said that being an intelligence analyst is harder than jumping out of airplanes (a reference to the covert side of CIA) because the stakes are so high. And it's because the stakes are so high that analytic tradecraft is well defined, clearly codified, and recognized as the standard across all US intelligence services. Intelligent Analysis means trusting the process. The tradecraft of Intelligent Analysis, like any other craft, can be learned and practiced.

- It's a well-tested conscious and deliberate process to deliver actionable intelligence that meets known audience requirements.

- Intelligent Analysis does not make predictions—the term conjures up guessing—but rather the most likely outcome is based on what is known at the time using a methodical approach that is transparent. The argument is evidence-based. It is easy to follow, the assessment is defensible, and the process used to develop the assessment is repeatable—and used every time.

- Data fuels Intelligent Analysis. It's collected and arrayed in tables, charts, and graphs to identify changes in trends and patterns that impact the audience's near- and long-term priority issues. Data establishes a baseline understanding that is key to establishing what is known and explained in the B.L.U.F.'s first four elements. (Aside from Intelligence Community Directives from the Office of the Director of National Intelligence, this chapter draws on multiple sources: Gartin, 2019; Petersen, 2011; Davis, 1997; Pfeffer and Sutton, 2006; Taleb, 2008).

Intelligent Analysis Is an End-to-End Process

Intelligent Analysis mirrors what the US intelligence services call the "intelligence cycle." Figure 6 provides a high-level overview of the flow.

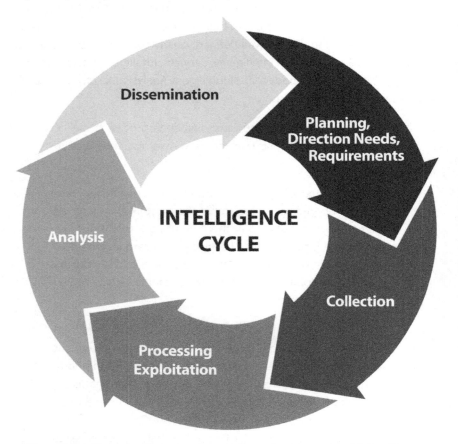

Figure 6. Intelligent Analysis transforms information into actionable intelligence.

Note that the cycle starts with known audience requirements (Planning and Direction) that determine what needs to be collected (or selected from databases) to answer specific questions. Analysis is where Intelligent Analysis transforms the information into actionable intelligence (Dissemination). And the cycle never ends because the assessment generates more and different questions. For example:

- Local law enforcement working on counter-narcotics wants to know if recent arrests indicate a shift in drug trafficking to another neighborhood.

- A pension manager wants due diligence conducted on a potential investment fund.

- A supply chain expert wants to know if new vendors have robust IT system security.

- A board of directors has asked for a risk assessment ahead of a possible merger.

- Insurance executives want to assess the risk of investing in real estate funds in a new area of the country.

- Senior managers in a large telecom company want to assess the risks of moving into emerging markets.

Intelligent Analysis gives you a process that can help analysts consistently bring important value added to their organizations.

Well-Validated Standards Define Good Intelligent Analysis

Intelligent Analysis adheres to the same standards that US intelligence services have followed for years. The Office of Director of National Intelligence most recently memorialized the standards in 2007 and updated them in 2015. They apply to written assessments, oral presentations, and graphics. These standards are the basis for training intelligence analysts across the US intelligence services and have long since migrated overseas to counterparts.

The CIA was the first to develop the matrix, but it has been adopted and adapted across intelligence agencies. Each agency may express them differently, but the standards themselves are fixed. Figure 7 on the next page is a composite drawn from different matrices. The bold and shaded text is explained below.

Message	Value Added	Argumenta-tion	Effective Structure	Presentation
Is relevant and enables audience decision-making	*Is accurate and timely*	*Body of analysis and evidence logically supports key judgments*	Selected format effectively communicates message to intended audience	Distinguishes between assumptions, evidence, and judgments
Main assessment is prominent and clear	Provides necessary context and anticipates a client's question	Quality of sourcing, information, and expertise clearly articulated	One main point per section, and one prominent topic sentence per paragraph	Tells a concise and consistent storyline
Assessments are neither obvious nor premature	Is collaborative, capturing regional, functional, and community analytic inputs	Expresses rationale for confidence level in judgments	Sub-bullets consistent with the paragraph to which they are attached	Uses precise language, avoiding ambiguous terms and jargon
Answers the Key Intelligence Question	Includes mitigation strategies as needed	Includes analysis of alternatives and captures differing views	Free of factual contradictions	Free of bias, value-laden terms, or advocacy
Explains the factors that changed the analytic line	Provides warning	Identifies gaps, potential impact on the assessment, and efforts to fill the gaps	Contains visuals that effectively convey or support the analysis	Free of grammatical errors, awkward constructions, typos, and misspellings

Figure 7. Written and oral analytic assessments, including graphics, must meet these standards every time.

Standards are high, reflecting a low tolerance for error and the hard critical thinking required to develop the elements of the lead paragraph. Subsequent chapters deal with each critical element. The table's legend is shown below in descending order of importance to Intelligent Analysis.

- **The standards in bold italics comprise the B.L.U.F.'s seven elements.** They are the most critical criteria that must be met before drafting begins. Reviewers cannot address shortfalls in this zone because the message, what must be conveyed to the audience up front, resides only in the analysts' heads. If standards are not met the assessment will be of little value. The shortfall is generally called a "[critical] thinking problem" because only the author can fix it.

- **The standards in light gray focus on good writing that would make the analysis more credible and the story easier to follow.** For example, "essential" qualities include a review of the text's structure and strong paragraph leads. Poorly written text is often understood as a sign that the assessment contains more substantial errors.

- **The standards in darker gray are required as appropriate.** For example, many readers welcome alternative views and mitigation strategies where analysts suggest actions that can shape a more favorable outcome. Warning has its own criteria that we will also look at later.

The qualities that define good Intelligent Analysis, and the methods used in this book map to the table.

Objectivity is non-negotiable. Analysts never bend to politics or avoid telling truth to power. Deliberately ignoring relevant reporting, skewing data, or excluding other perspectives makes the analysis suspect; it's easily spotted and violates analysts' fundamental value: their integrity. Even appearing to advocate an outcome will destroy your credibility, possibly for good, and can sow distrust of Intelligent Analysis more broadly. Don't do it. If you cannot resist being a cheering section for your audience, do something else. The media is replete with pundits masquerading as analysts; there is always room for one more. What was noted earlier bears repeating: Intelligent Analysis forces you to slow down, encourages you to be more deliberate and conscious about how you craft the assessments, and shifts the discussions from personalities to the data. Biases, emotions, and competing agendas are toxic to good decision-making.

The audience's agenda drives the process. The intelligence cycle underscores that the audience must be the starting and end points for Intelligent Analysis. They expect you to know the high priority near- and longer-term issues that drive their days, what they need from you, and the timing. Developing such close relationships can be challenging but it is central to the analyst's job. Each assessment produced for the audience is an opportunity to strengthen or undermine that relationship. Otherwise, you are firing blanks.

The argument is persuasive and easy to track. Clear writing and the analytic process are inseparable. Intelligent Analysis requires clear sourcing, and grammatically correct prose strengthens the assessment's credibility. The structure expands on the lead paragraph, making the message easier to track in longer assessments.

Visuals reinforce main points and enhance impact. Graphics, tables, maps, and charts must adhere to the same standards of quality as written and oral presentations. They must convey a clear message, be easily understood, and be easy to read. They should also comply with requirements for access to visually impaired readers such as those with color blindness.

Follow the Process

Your audience lives in a world of ambiguity and uncertainty every day and they trust you, or can come to trust you, to provide actionable intelligence that can help them clearly see risks and opportunities. What you say or write can either matter and add value to the organization's mission or not. They need consistency in the quality of the analysis and how it is presented, its timeliness, and its focus on their priorities and relevance to their issues. They trust that it is objective and complete, every time. These demands are what make Intelligent Analysis so critical. And it is why this book so frequently reminds analysts to follow the process. The world's best analysts who serve in the US intelligence services have validated Intelligent Analysis over decades of work. Skipping steps or telling yourself that you are ready to write when you are not will leave you where you are now, staring at the paper or writing assessments that are ignored. Worse, the audience may make a decision based on what they assume to be an accurate assessment.

Don't settle. Own what you write. Nothing leaves your desk that deserves less than an "A". Only you know what needs to be said. Don't expect someone else to fix it.

Meeting these standards consistently is hard work and not for everyone. More than anything else, years of experience and training analysts underscore that success and enjoyment of analytic work is a matter of temperament. Here are some of the qualities that over time have proven essential. Most notably, successful analysts:

- Display insatiable curiosity. They are relentless in searching for answers and asking questions.

- Share credit; they don't need to be a star.

- Never bends to politics. Integrity is everything.

- Show intellectual courage. Make sure your tradecraft is solid and then defend it based on what you report.

- Work well under intense pressure and short deadlines.

- Collaborate, leveraging expertise and recognizing everyone's value.

- Commit to a mission, whether public or private sector. Make your work matter!

- Build deep expertise.

- Welcome and give constructive feedback. Always look to be better and help others improve as well.

- Adapt. Audiences and requirements change. Each change is a new opportunity to build an important relationship.

- Show humility. Admit mistakes and remain open to other perspectives.

- Listen attentively, respectfully, and critically.

- Stay professional, always. No raised voices or whining. Focus on the data.

And have fun. It has to be part of the vocabulary. Intelligent Analysis is hard work—a vocation, actually—and when it becomes drudgery, it will be time to move on.

EXERCISE:
How Clear Is the Message?

This exercise asks you to measure the quality of an assessment, in this case a short article from *The Economist*, against the criteria that define good Intelligent Analysis as explained in this chapter. In particular, look at the most critical criteria from the analytical standards described above.

If you wish, you can start using your own work here, answering the same questions.

Instructions: Read the article from the perspective of a non-expert investor in rare vintage wine trying to decide if buying barrels of fine burgundy is a good investment. Then answer the questions at the end of the text.

Smoking Barrels: Amateur Buyers of Fine Burgundy Fear a Speculative Bubble
Investors are looking beyond Bordeaux
The Economist, January 3, 2019

EVERY year Berry Bros & Rudd, Britain's oldest wine merchant, issues a pocket-sized price list. Reading old copies makes amateurs of quality quaff want to time-travel. In 1909 a case of 12 bottles of Domaine de la Romanée-Conti 1891, Burgundy's most famous Grand Cru, cost 180 shillings (about £1,000, or $1,300, in today's money). In its historic London store, which opened in 1698, a single 18-year-old bottle of similar quality now sells for £25,000.

Fine wine is expensive to store, and its rarity and high transaction costs make it—oddly enough—an illiquid asset. Even so, its appreciation with age and perceived ability to diversify portfolios have made it popular with investors over the past two decades. The value of wine exchanged yearly between decisionmakers, connoisseurs and collectors—the secondary market—has quadrupled to $4bn since 2000, says Justin Gibbs of Liv-ex, a wine-trading platform. He reckons that just 15% of those buying wine on his website are doing so to drink it. The rest see it as a store of value.

Fine wines are traded privately, at auctions or through exchanges like Liv-ex, where members bid for listed wines. The equivalent of an initial public offering comes when estates release their latest vintages. The wine world also has asset managers, which buy and sell hundreds of cases on behalf of clients in the hope of turning a profit. Britain is a big trading hub, notably because it offers the ability to store wine free of customs and VAT provided it's kept in one of the few taxman-approved warehouses. Many professional buyers hold their stock under the same huge vaults. Updating records is sometimes all it takes to transfer ownership.

Investing in wine has long meant buying Bordeaux. But that is changing: the French region now accounts for 60% of secondary transactions, down from 95% in 2011. The new picks have star appeal. Bordeaux prices have done well in the past three years, rising by a third. But the value of fine Burgundy has more than doubled, according to the Liv-ex 1000 index.

One reason is that greater price transparency has boosted buyers' confidence. Fine wines, which don't generate cash flows, cannot be valued using financial metrics such as price-to-earnings ratios. But exchanges and websites like Wine Searcher, which gathers merchant quotes from around the world, provide reference points. Apps that collect reviews from critics and decisionmakers also help; so, do gadgets to improve traceability (though fakes remain a problem). Some of this cash finds its way to new terroirs.

Investors are becoming more sophisticated, too. Chinese buyers, whose thirst for Bordeaux kept prices afloat through the financial crisis, fled the region after 2012, when a crackdown on corruption meant demand for luxury goods dried up. Many have since turned to Burgundy. Most wine-investment funds, which in the 2000s managed €350m ($396m), almost all of it invested in Bordeaux, went bust when the market tanked. Such outfits have since re-formed, trying harder to diversify.

Recent currency shifts have made top crus (Burgundy wine) a relative bargain. Burgundy was already cheaper than Bordeaux, and a dollar rally after 2015 has put the region on American and Asian buyers' radars (the Hong Kong dollar is pegged to the greenback). Italian, Californian, and other French regions have also become fashionable, says Philip Staveley of Amphora, a wine-portfolio manager. But the best Burgundy is produced in tiny volumes. Chateau Margaux, a Bordeaux star, puts out 11,000 cases a year; Domaine de la Romanée-Conti makes 450. That amplifies price movements.

Experts fear a bubble. "Everyone tells us it's getting absurd," says Philippe Masset, a wine scholar. Younger vintages have become pricier than older ones—the wine equivalent of a yield-curve inversion. The Burgundy region gained 8% in November, while all others plateaued. Whether that lasts may depend on the value-for-money of the vintage released this month. But for now, investors see the glass half-full.

QUESTIONS

1. **What is the main point you take away from the article?**

---

2. **Was that message easy to identify?** Why or why not?

---

3. When you are finished, answer this question: **Were you able to determine if you should jump into Burgundy wines?** Why or why not?

---

4. **What other information might help you make a more informed decision?**

---

5. **Draft a sentence that you think better captures the message for busy readers.**

CHAPTER THREE

Tailor Analysis to the Target Audience

"Every intelligence product must be rooted in a strong understanding of the audience it is written for."

—Martin Petersen,
*What I Learned in 40 Years of Doing
Intelligence Analysis for US Foreign Policymakers*

SUMMARY

Main Points

- Trust is critical for building relationships with your audience.

- Senior executives have their own networks, so trust between analysts and their target audiences is not automatic. It is often hard to develop trust, but it is easy to lose and the loss is permanent.

- Senior executives may know you only from your analytic work, so you are always in the room with them even if you never meet.

- The intelligence cycle illustrates the centrality of the audience's requirements as the main driver in Intelligent Analysis.

Key Takeaways

- Focusing on the audience's operating environment and near- and longer-term priority issues is essential to building trust and developing a service mentality.

- It is the analysts' job to build these relationships. Without this knowledge you will likely waste time and resources, and your work be ignored because it's late and/or irrelevant.

- As an exercise, the chapter introduces two frameworks that require analysts to be more deliberate in identifying their target audience and to understand that stakeholders looking at the same issue may have different decision-making requirements regarding the same event or development.

- The Audience Assessment Framework helps you become more deliberate in understanding their day-to-day operating environment.

- The Audience Requirements Assessment Framework helps you home in on their short- and long-term intelligence requirements.

CHAPTER 3:
Tailor Analysis to the Target Audience

"Every intelligence product must be rooted in a strong understanding of the audience it is written for. In a service mentality, the focus is on the consumer—the consumer of our services—and specifically on how best to meet the consumer's needs. It's not about the author or the producing component; it's about the recipient."
—**Martin Petersen,** *What I Learned in 40 Years of Doing Intelligence Analysis for US Foreign Policymakers*

Goal: To better understand why expertise, knowledge of the audience, and a service mentality are essential to building the trust that will determine the strength of the relationship.

Objectives

At the end of this chapter, analysts will be better able to:

- Explain how trust fuels the strength of the audience-analyst relationship.

- Understand that it is the analyst's responsibility to help build that relationship.

- Describe the importance of a service mentality in supporting your target audience.

- Demonstrate the use of two assessment tools that can help analysts be more deliberate in building that relationship and see that there are likely multiple different audiences for the same issue.

Trust Drives the Audience-Analyst Relationship

In Intelligent Analysis the relationship between the audience and analysts is the start and end point of the analytic process, and trust fuels it. Audiences likely have multiple other sources of information, and for analysts to compete for attention they must demonstrate a clear understanding of their operating environment and the near-and long-term intelligence requirements. The audience needs to come to expect that analytic assessments will be tightly focused on these requirements and timed to support their schedules and that work is objective, evidence based, and clearly written. The book borrows the term *service mentality* from the commercial world to describe this single-minded emphasis on the audience. It looks at analysts' responsibility to build this trust from two perspectives: knowing the audience's operating environment and intelligence requirements.

If this sounds like a full-time job, it is because sustaining trust is a never-ending process, but this will give analysts meaning to their work and potentially a seat at the table when decisions are made. One way to think about the analyst-audience relationship is that analysts are their audience's eyes and ears, functioning like a trip wire, reporting new information that for better or worse impacts their issues now or points to a trend over the horizon that could affect the organization. When you provide that support, you are in the room or on the plane with them even if you never meet them. Your assessments speak for themselves. It's what makes the work rewarding and why everything must deserve an "A" when you hit the send button. There are few second chances.

Building these critical relationships, however, can be challenging because of who the audience is or their backgrounds. Senior and especially executive decision-makers almost always bring their own networks, if not staff, with them. If they already know the business, they likely already have access to multiple sources of information, including friends, former colleagues, outside experts, or those that brought them into the organization. They may not, however, know anything about what you do or what value you can bring or even how to contact you, especially if they have never worked with analysts. And because they are so busy, they are not waiting for your golden insights, so it's up to you to take the initiative to establish contact. Understand that, even with their own networks, they are unlikely to have access to what you are best equipped to provide: objective, evidence-based analysis, straight talk and "bad news" delivered carefully. There is only a small window, however, to make your case. And it all starts with really understanding their world and what they need to be successful.

Two Frameworks Sharpen Audience Focus

Intelligence Analysis's critical upfront work begins with knowing specifically who you are serving and what they need from you. Understanding their operating environments—what they worry about most—and what they need from analysts now and over the long-term makes you proactive and relevant, providing real value added to the organization's mission. Ignorance leaves analysts sidelined and the work stops being fun. These two frameworks push analysts to think more deliberately about the target audience for the assessment selected to work on through the rest of the book.

- **The Audience Assessment Framework** helps you become more deliberate in understanding their day-to-day operating environment.

- **The Audience Requirements Assessment Framework** helps you home in on their short- and long-term Intelligence requirements.

As you look at the range of the audience's responsibilities, you will see that while they work together, they will look at the development or event from different perspectives that will have different intelligence requirements.

Exercise: Assess Audience Operating Environments

Let's start with an example.

Perspective: You are in an organization which is trying to decide whether to bid on a large contract procurement. As the senior business intelligence analyst with deep expertise on the industry, you are best positioned to evaluate the proposition from the perspectives and equities of the multiple stakeholders involved. Figure 8 is a completed framework that can be a model for the exercise. Note in column 1 that the decision makers hold specific positions in the company, and they will be part of the decision. One size will not fit all: one development but multiple interested stakeholders and perspectives. An explanation of each column follows.

1. Identify audience members.	2. To whom does audience member report?	3. What is their day like?	4. What are their most important concerns?	5. How much do they know about you?
Senior Executive/ Decision Maker	-Stockholders -Board -Clients	-Attend/chair meetings -Strategic decision-making -Near/long-term planning -Personnel development -Budget -Marketing	-Win percentage -Compliance -Shareholder value -What's next	-Seen your assessments but not always useful -Never worked with analysts
Chief Risk Officer	-CEO -Lawyers -Accountants -Board -Regulators	-Oversee due diligence -Advise audience -Assure compliance -Develop/ implement risk mgt policy	-Competing demands, buyer, seller, regulators -What am I missing? -Insider threats	-New -Doesn't even know where you sit
Senior Director for Business Development	-VP Business Development	-Review proposals -Gather business intelligence -Gather competitive intelligence -Assess new opportunities -Proposal budget	Overconfident stakeholders -Get the price right -Competition -Staffing	-Well known but no sense of potential to add value
Senior Business Analyst	-The entire management chain	-Multiple demands -Unclear instructions -What to write -Product content	-Missed opportunities -Irrelevance -Connecting with audience	

Figure 8. The Audience Assessment Framework identifies the target audiences.
The explanation starts with Column 1.

- **Column 1: *Whom do you directly support?*** This is just a notional list of whom you want to cultivate, identified by position. Counterparts are not your audience. Look higher up the organization's hierarchy.

- **Column 2: *To whom does the audience report?*** In many instances, what you provide your audience is destined for the person they report to. For example, a risk assessment of a bank proposal may be just about the bank or it may feed into a larger assessment of a possible merger or acquisition. Knowing that you can alter the assessment may also feed into an oral briefing for a more senior audience. The key here is to be sure you know how to help your direct supervisor be successful.

- **Column 3: *What is their day like?*** Obviously, they are busy but busy with what, specifically? For example, do they have time to read reports, sort through data, and set priorities, or is most of their day scheduled or unpredictable?

- **Column 4: *What are their most important concerns?*** What do they worry most about? Generally, it's surprises or risks to personnel, unwelcome publicity, an unexpected event, or being blindsided.

- **Column 5: *How much does the audience know about you?*** Unless the target audience is among the few that come to their position with some exposure to intelligence, such as what you do and the value you can add to their work, you are probably a mystery. And this is your problem, not theirs. "Analyst" to them may well be a vague term that conjures up a fortune teller capable of predicting what's next. And they are highly unlikely to understand that you practice a unique skill set. They might even think of you as simply an academic or an extra hand to be to be used as needed.

EXERCISE:
Identify Your Own Audience

Using the example as a model, complete the template for at least your two, but no more than three, most important targets. They may be ones you are already supporting or those you want to connect with. At least one should be your assessment's audience.

Think hard about whom you list and answer the questions carefully, because this will be the basis for the rest of the exercises

Be as specific as you can. Telling yourself they have full schedules might be correct, but that insight does not really help you sort out who needs intelligence support.

Use the boxes or the space below for your answers or complete the framework on your computer.

Don't make up answers. Blanks are part of the exercise.

1. Identify audience members.	2. To whom does audience member report?	3. What is their day like?	4. What are their most important concerns?	5. How much do they know about you?
Optional Third				

Whom do you directly support?

Audience Member 1: _____

Audience Member 2: _____

Audience Member 3 (Optional): _____

To whom does the audience member report?

Audience Member 1: _____

Audience Member 2: _____

Audience Member 3: _____

What is their day like? Describe it.

Audience Member 1: _____

Audience Member 2: _____

Audience Member 3: _____

What are their most important concerns?

Audience Member 1: _____

Audience Member 2: _____

Audience Member 3: _____

How much does the audience know about you?

Audience Member 1: _____

Audience Member 2: _____

Audience Member 3: _____

Now ask yourself:

How easy was it for you to identify your audience?

_____

What areas did you know most about; least about?

_____

What steps can you take to better answer these questions?

_____

To what extent does this exercise change how you think about your audience?

_____

Before moving on, think for a minute and list two or three words that describe the world your audience inhabits every day. See my example below.

1. _____

2. _____

3. _____

Here are some of the ways you might characterize the world your audience inhabits every day:

- Filled with uncertainty
- Filled with unknowns
- Filled with risk
- Filled with complexities
- Filled with problems to solve . . but also filled with potential
- Filled with unknown opportunities
- Filled with alternatives and choices

So, to serve them well analysts need to understand their audience's world first before writing.

Audience Requirements Assessment Framework Identifies Priorities

Knowing what actionable intelligence the audience needs is the second half of the equation. It's what makes you proactive and relevant. Figure 9 shows the framework that, when completed, will confirm the audience's near- and longer-term priority intelligence requirements. They must be updated regularly with audience assistance, sometimes as often as weekly, to make sure you are focused on what matters. One development but multiple interested stakeholders, perspectives, and requirements.

Perspective:
A large contractor is trying to decide whether to bid on a project. The senior business analyst has figured out the audience but is not sure how go about determining their individual requirements and decides to use the Audience Assessment Framework to gather the data and fill in the gaps in his knowledge. The analyst assumes the first three columns are carryovers from the completed audience identification framework.

1. Identify audience members.	2. To whom does audience member report?	3. What is their day like?
Senior Executive	-Stockholders -Board -Clients	-Attend/chair meetings -Strategic decisions -Near/long- term planning -Personnel -Budget -Marketing
Chief Risk Officer	-CEO -Board of Directors	-React to questions -Provide assessments -Meet with CEO -Insider threats
Senior Director for Business Development	-VP Business Development	-Review proposals -Gather business intelligence -Gather competitive intelligence -Assess new opportunities -Monitor proposal budget

Chart continues on next page

Figure 9. Knowing requirements is the other half . . .

4. What are their highest priority issues??	5. What are their long-term issues?	6. How can I learn more about the audience?
-Winning -Protect his position -Avoid scandal -The next bid -Hiring, retaining key staff -Changes in business climate -No surprises -Manage board	-Possible acquisitions -Monitor political domestic foreign climate -Track economic forecasts -Ensure compliance -Plan for climate change -Protect brand	-Work with management chain to learn calendar -Meet with staff assistance -Network
-Report on current risks -Warn of new threats	-Reduce systemic vulnerabilities	-Work with your supervisor -Meet with CTO periodically, see his calendar
-Winning -Pick next contract to bid	-Build more integrated due diligence team	-Meet with counterparts to start on guidance for next products

. . . of the audience knowledge equation.

Here are the explanations for columns 4–6.

- **Column 4: What are the audience's highest priority issues:** Looking over the next 30 to 60 days, what are their most immediate requirements?

- **Column 5: What are their long-term issues:** What are their more strategic priorities with a horizon ranging from six months to a year and beyond?

- **Column 6: How can I learn more about my decision maker:** Not a time to be shy. Team up. Use your supervisor and set up lunch or breaks with counterparts. Find out who knows the schedules and look for changes; this will position you to write to their agendas.

EXERCISE:
Identify Audience Intelligence Requirements

Instructions:

- The blank chart below shows the requirements framework to complete.

- Use no more than two potential target audiences for your project from the last exercise. The example can serve as a model to help you fill in the framework. You have already completed the two shaded columns, so just enter that information as is.

- Leave blank what you don't know. Be as specific as you can, but don't guess. It's part of the exercise.

- Note the differences between the two audiences as they look at the same event or development. At the end of the exercise, you will be asked to choose the one target audience for your project.

1. Identify audience members.	2. To whom does audience member report?	3. What is their day like?

4. What are their highest priority issues??	5. What are their long-term issues?	6. How can I learn more about the audience?

Identify your decision makers (enter from last exercise):
Audience Member 1: _____
 Audience Member 2: _____

To whom do your audiences report (enter from last exercise):
Audience Member 1: _____
Audience Member 2: _____

Describe your audiences' world (enter from last exercise):
Audience Member 1: _____
Audience Member 2: _____

List their highest priority issues:
Audience Member 1: _____
Audience Member 2: _____

List their longer-term issues:
Audience Member 1: _____
Audience Member 2: _____

How you can learn more about your decision maker:
Audience Member 1: _____
Audience Member 2: _____

Pick Your Target: Summarize Knowns, Unknowns about Your Primary Target Audience

Identify your assessment's primary target audience: who will be best positioned to act on your Intelligent Analysis? Then answer these five questions:

- What is the target's name and/or specific position?

- How would you describe their operating environment?

- What are your target's near- and longer-term priorities?

- What are the gaps in your knowledge of the target?

- How might you fill these gaps?

Armed with this knowledge you can be proactive in meeting their require-ments: what they need, the timing, and the format. Trust is built and the work becomes rewarding and fun.

CHAPTER FOUR

Bottom Line Up Front Leads Assessment and Delivers Actionable Intelligence

> "I have to have a lead, or I can't write anything. I have to have my first sentence, because that's my whole piece. That's the tone, that says what is this piece about, it's the theme, the thing by which everything hangs. If I don't have that first sentence, I just can't keep going forward."
>
> —Susan Trausch
> *The Boston Globe*

SUMMARY

Main Points

- In Intelligent Analysis, the B.L.U.F. is the tightly for-matted lead paragraph that conveys actionable intel-ligence to the audience.

- Required B.L.U.F. elements: from what's known to what's ahead, conveyed in five to seven sentences.

  1. *What?* What development or event has prompt-ed the question?

  2. *Why now?* What is precipitating the event or development?

  3. *How does it work?* Is there a process or terminol-ogy to be explained?

  4. *What's the impact so far?* What has happened because of the event?

  5. *What's ahead?* What's the "so what" for the audience?

  6. *What are the implications?* What's "the so what of the so what" that explains the importance of what's ahead?

  7. *What can be done to mitigate risks or exploit opportunities?*

- The B.L.U.F. can be readily expanded into a longer as-sessment; each element can, for example, become a separate paragraph or section.

Key Takeaways

■ The B.L.U.F. must convey the message the same way every time.

■ This chapter only introduces the B.L.U.F. Subsequent chapters explain how each element is completed.

For senior executives, this chapter shows what to expect from Intelligent Analysis.

The book walks analysts and decision support staff through each B.L.U.F. element with explanations and exercises, building the project's lead paragraph at the end of each chapter.

CHAPTER 4:
Bottom Line Up Front Leads Assessment,
Delivers Actionable Intelligence

"I have to have a lead, or I can't write anything. I have to have my first sentence, because that's my whole piece. That's the tone, that says what is this piece about, it's the theme, the thing by which everything hangs. If I don't have that first sentence, I just can't keep going forward."
—**Susan Trausch,** *The Boston Globe*

Goal: To provide context that will explain Intelligence Analysis's emphasis on the Bottom Line Up Front (B.L.U.F.) as the required format to succinctly convey a complete message to your audience and set the stage for subsequent chapters that explain how to develop its component parts.

Objectives

At the end of this chapter, analysts will be better able to:

- Explain the importance of the B.L.U.F. in Intelligent Analysis.

- Understand how the B.L.U.F. framework includes all seven key elements.

- Understand how the B.L.U.F. can be the basis for structuring longer assessments.

Note: In Intelligent Analysis the B.L.U.F. is the vehicle to convey the message. This chapter is intended only to introduce the B.L.U.F. and its component parts, so just focus on how it is structured and the component parts.. The book returns to completion of the related exercises as subsequent chapters present the mechanics of developing each required element. For senior executives, this chapter shows what to expect from Intelligent Analysis. For their part, analysts will learn and practice developing the separate elements of the B.L.U.F., and they will develop an early draft of the lead paragraph for the project. There may be unfamiliar terms. Be patient. Each chapter goes into depth on one or more of the seven elements and includes returning to the draft for refinements which needs to be done in any event—you are never done. Think about each element as you work through the guide.

Constructing the B.L.U.F. Is Methodical, Demanding Work

A well-constructed B.L.U.F. conveys actionable intelligence in a fixed format, comprising three closely related parts that together send a consistent message (Cariens, 2012; Major, 2009).

1. The B.L.U.F., which includes all seven of the message's required elements.
2. A summary of the message, in the form of an inference that leads the paragraph and sets out the actionable intelligence (discussed in chapter 6).
3. An analytic title, that captures the inference's message in no more than 10 words (discussed in chapter 11).

In Intelligent Analysis, these three components are the foundation of every written assessment and oral presentation of any length. Its succinctness and consistency deliver actionable intelligence in a clear message that explains the "what" and the "so what" and why it matters without wading through text. This is no ordinary first paragraph, but the product of hard thinking, and only the analyst as the expert can do this work.

To once again review the deliberate thinking that goes into crafting the B.L.U.F. construct, we want to emphasize that it's the road to a clear message. It's fixed and unchanging. The paragraph's consistency, predictability, and how it tells a complete story, are its most important strengths. The audience knows what to expect every time. Done well, the trust between audience and analyst grows. The B.L.U.F. flows:

From what's known . . .

1. **What?** What development or event has prompted the question? The development, new data, or change that needs to be reported based on the audience's near- and longer- term requirements. For example, reporting over the last two weeks points to signs of a drought.

2. **Why now?** What is precipitating the event of development? Why is it happening now? All changes that can answer this question can be expressed as a:

- **Trend:** the development reflects an increase or decrease (or not); what does the data say? For example, measures of an epidemic, unemployment, risk, or auto sales.

- **Pattern:** the development reflects a shift in what had been predictable behavior. For example, ride sharing replaces car ownership, or an airline long operating in one region opens new routes; opioids spread geographically and across user demographics.

- **Relationship:** the development establishes that an event or action was a direct cause that makes another event happen. A change in X (cause) produces a change in Y (effect). Or think of it this way: the cause = why it happened and the effect = what happened. For example, the appointment of a new CEO (cause) and needed reforms boosted profits (effect), or the perceived fraudulent presidential election (cause) and massive demonstrations took place (effect).

3. **How does it work?** Is there a process or terminology to be explained? This element is included when the development is a process or flow that requires explanation of how it works. For example, your decision maker may be unfamiliar with certain types of legal or illegal financial transactions, the use of technology in medical diagnosis, or the mechanics of bitcoin and money laundering.

4. **What's the impact so far?** What has happened because of the development or event? The impact explains the size, scope, and outcome to date. For example, the post-election demonstrations have led to dozens of deaths, or a company is preparing for an acquisition, or a family looks at a potential move.

The impact is data driven and with responses to B.L.U.F. elements one through three comprise what's known and the basis for the look ahead.

**. . .To the unknown: assessment of what's next (the "so what")
and why it matters to the audience (the "so what of the so what")**

5. ***What's ahead?*** What's the "so what" for the audience? The most likely outcome, or the "so what," is based on what can be inferred (more, less, better, worse, no change) from what is known. It includes an estimated level of probability that the event or development will take place. For example:

- The competition's determination to cut their prices to the bone and our determination to maintain our market share will very likely require significant internal shifts to sustain demand.

6. ***What are the implications?*** What's the "so what of the so what" that explains the importance of what's ahead—why should it matter to the audience? For example:

- The challenges from emerging competitors and our current workforce structure will very likely cut into sales and require a redeployment of sales representatives and push our company to consider shifting production overseas.

7. ***What can be done*** to mitigate risks and exploit opportunities? Again, based on expertise, suggested mitigation strategies and indications of their effectiveness flow from the implications. For example:

- Over the next year deployed sales representatives and changes in production should allow the company to reduce costs by 10 percent and boost sales at least six percent over the same time period.

To Start, Break Old Habits: The B.L.U.F.'s Pyramid Points Up

Figure 10 shows two very different structures for whatever you are writing, but only one, the B.L.U.F., meets the requirement for how to answer the audience's question. Placing the bottom line on the bottom, or B.L.O.B., means a long journey to find your message. It's common in academic journals and college writing classes, but in the world of Intelligent Analysis, imagine your audience having to search for the B.L.U.F. It just won't work; too much to wade through. In the B.L.O.B., the lead is a typical topic sentence followed by the proof that leads to a conclusion. In the B.L.U.F., the inference leads the paragraph followed by supporting evidence in the seven B.L.U.F. elements.

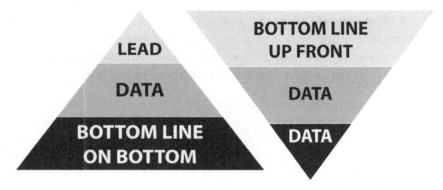

Figure 10. Intelligent Analysis bans the B.L.O.B. and embraces the B.L.U.F.

The B.L.O.B. is all about the writer; the B.L.U.F. is all about the audience. Be a servant.

EXERCISE
B.L.O.B. or B.L.U.F.: Find the Main Point

Here is a short article based on an auto sales forecast for 2019.

Perspective: You are an analyst for an investment firm where you are responsible for tracking and assessing auto industry sales and production forecasts, making recommendations for investments, and reporting them to your department manager for review.

Audience: The investment firm's managing director charged with following the automobile industry

KIQ: This is the question you have been asked to answer:

To what extent is NADA's forecast consistent with other reporting and assessments of factors that will impact auto sales and auto manufacturers' production decisions over the next year?

Instructions:

Read the article on auto sales and production and answer the questions at the end.

Remember that this forecast would be of interest to multiple stakeholders in the firm, but the decision maker is the department head who looks to you for actionable intelligence analysis they can take to senior decision makers.

NADA Forecasts 16.8 Million New-Vehicle Sales in 2019

New-vehicle sales are on pace to reach 17 million units in 2018, which would mark the fourth straight year of U.S. auto sales above 17 million units

Charles Cyrill, NADA Director of Public Relations, TYSONS, Va.

December 13, 2018

The National Automobile Dealers Association, a trade group representing U.S. franchised new-car dealerships, today released its annual sales forecast for new light vehicles in 2019.

"We're forecasting sales of 16.8 million new cars and light trucks in 2019," said Patrick Manzi, NADA senior economist, at an industry briefing. "This would represent a falloff in sales of about 1.1 percent compared to 2018."

Based on a strong November, new-vehicle sales are expected to reach 17 million units in 2018, which would mark the fourth straight year of U.S. auto sales above 17 million units.

"This was unexpected. We were expecting sales to fall off a little more than they have this year, but then the new tax law was passed which put more money in the pockets of decisionmakers and they certainly purchased new vehicles at dealer showrooms," Manzi added. "The majority of these sales, following the trend of past years, have been light trucks, such as crossovers, pickups and SUVs."

NADA Chairman Wes Lutz, president of Extreme Dodge-Chrysler-Jeep-Ram in Jackson, Mich., who provided a dealer perspective on the state of auto retailing during the briefing, added that sales of 16.8 million new vehicles would still be a robust year in 2019 but was concerned about "price creeping" that could take some decisionmakers out the market.

"If incentives continue to go down and interest rates go up, it will put tremendous pressure on decisionmakers with rising monthly payments," Lutz added. "The level of interest rates moving forward will be a wildcard."

In 2018, decisionmakers continued to abandon car segments. Light trucks are on track to account for about 70 percent of sales, while cars will account for nearly 30 percent of sales. In 2017, the ratio was 64.5 percent light trucks and 35.5 percent cars. About 10 years ago, the sales mix consisted of 48 percent light trucks and 52 percent cars.

"One of the main factors for this shift has been continued low oil and gasoline prices and the fact that crossover utility vehicles are nearly as fuel efficient as their sedan counterparts. And we've seen fuel economy increases across the board, not just on crossovers but also traditional SUVs and pickups," Manzi said. "We also expect gasoline prices to remain relatively low in 2019, not as low as present but still low enough not to cause a panic and a decisionmaker shift back to the car market."

Incentive spending, on average, per unit was down in November 2018 compared to the same month a year ago, according to industry sources.

"We've seen more discipline from auto manufacturers with their production this year. They have properly aligned production with demand and as a result have relied less on incentives, although some incentives applied on less popular segments may spike in December 2018 as well as fleet sales at the end of the year," Manzi added. "We expect incentives to continue to fall and automakers to remain disciplined in 2019."

Manzi, who agreed with Lutz, added that a significant headwind for decisionmakers is rising interest rates for new-vehicle financing.

"Depending on what source you look at, average interest rates on new-vehicle financing have risen 60 to 70 basis points from 2017 through the third quarter of 2018. That has really driven up the cost of borrowing," he said. "We expect interest rates to continue to rise. There has been some speculation that the frequency of rate increases may slow."

The Federal Reserve Board is expected to raise rates at its meeting in December 2018. One or two more rate increases are likely during the early half of 2019 and then rates are expected to hold steady.

A positive trend for both decisionmakers and new-car dealerships has been the growth in manufacturer-backed certified pre-owned (CPO) sales. CPO sales are up 2.2 percent through November 2018.

"The price gap in average monthly payments between new and used vehicles is widening. Decisionmakers, even those with stellar credit, are doing the math and many will choose to buy used vehicles from new-car dealerships, which are uniquely positioned and qualified to sell CPO vehicles," Manzi said. "Off-lease returns to dealerships are expected to peak in 2019 following record leasing in 2016. That means more CPO sales for franchised dealers."

Lutz, who sells two used vehicles for every new model sold at his dealership, added that rising transaction prices in the new-vehicle market will result in more decisionmakers shopping for used vehicles.

"There's an abundance of late-model, off-lease vehicles returning to dealerships, which offers decisionmakers an alternative to higher monthly payments on a new vehicle," Lutz said.

Manzi also provided an outlook of the macroeconomic factors that will impact auto retailing in 2019.

"The tax cuts signed into law in 2018 provided a significant boost to the overall economy. It likely resulted in GDP growth of 3 percent for the year, pushed average employment growth up to 206,000 jobs per month and unemployment down below 4 percent, and increased new-vehicle sales," he said. "We're not going to have that again in 2019. That's one of the main reasons we're expecting new-vehicle sales to fall off slightly."

NADA expects GDP growth of about 2.5 percent in 2019 and then a return to a long-term trend growth rate of about 2 percent or slightly lower.

"We expect the rate of job growth to slow to between 150,000 to 170,000 jobs per month," Manzi said. "And there's still more room for the unemployment rate to fall and wages to rise."

Lutz added that new-car dealers are generally optimistic about 2019 and excited about changes in technology from advanced safety features, improved fuel economy and especially vehicle electrification.

There are 270 million vehicles on the road today with gasoline combustion engines, Lutz said. New-car dealers would like to replace all of them.

Answer the Following Questions

Identify and write down or mark what you see as the main point(s) of the article.

_____

_____

_____

Is this article a B.L.O.B. or a B.L.U.F.? _____?

Why?_____

_____

_____

Recalling your understanding of the audience, how effectively would it support the decision maker ahead of the meeting?

_____

_____

_____

Craft a new lead sentence that you think captures the main message more effectively.

_____

_____

_____

_____

A Model to Follow: B.L.U.F. Framework Channels Your Thinking

Figure 11 based on this article below is a model B.L.U.F. to follow. It uses the same audience and KIQ set out above. Recall:

The audience: The investment firm's managing director charged with following the automobile industry.

The question: To what extent is NADA's forecast consistent with other reporting and assessments of factors that will impact auto sales and auto manufacturers' production decisions over the next year?

Note how each element is structured and fully written out and how they flow from one element to the next in the lead paragraph.

	Auto Industry Adjusting Incentives, Production Ahead of Anticipated 2019 Sales Decline
Inference summarizes the B.L.U.F. (Note: crafting the inference is detailed in chapter 7.)	The NADA PR head says tax cuts prevented a steeper decline in auto sales in 2018, but with the bump gone, vehicle sales in 2019 will slip below 17 million vehicles for the first time in four years, which very likely means dealers and manufacturers will continue to recalibrate production targets and incentives as continuing shifts toward SUVs and trucks and rising prices and interest rates prompt renewed focus on used cars.
What?	A decline in sales has convinced manufacturers to reduce production and available incentives to cut costs.
Why now?	A combination of factors is driving down new car sales and increasing demand for used cars, including interest and price hikes and lower fuel costs that make SUVs, trucks, and crossovers attractive alternatives to new cars; unsettled trade policies compound risk to automakers.
How does it work?	Manufacturers have moved aggressively to protect profit margins, including cutting production and largely shifting small car production to non-US plants, and dealers have reduced buyer incentives.
What's the impact so far?	Market shifts are already apparent: light trucks are now accounting for 70 percent of sales and used car sales are up over 2 percent because of price creep and availability of late model leased cars.

	Auto Industry Adjusting Incentives, Production Ahead of Anticipated 2019 Sales Decline
What's ahead ("so what")?	Multiple other uncertain variables could further impact production and sales, including declining economic forecasts in China and South America, tariffs, and uncertainty in the outcome of trade talks.
What are the implications (the "so what of the so what")?	Automakers will have to hedge their production plans; dealers will have to look for ways to balance their inventories against costs. Changes in the production mix will impact auto workers. Incentive programs and discounts will shrink, especially in the truck market.
What can be done to mitigate risks and exploit opportunities?	In an uncertain environment, automakers can continue to hedge their bets, shutting down weak dealerships and shifting product mix in ways that will impact production facilities in the US. Dealers can reduce their inventories and, with incentive programs shrinking, dealers have more flexibility in growing their service business.

Figure 11. The B.L.U.F. always includes these seven components. Always.

Exercise: Start Thinking About Your Own B.L.U.F.

Recall that at this point we are just introducing the B.L.U.F. framework—why it matters and how it is structured. For now, study the framework and the introduction to the lead inference, which is an integral part of the B.L.U.F. that follows the blank template. We will return to the framework as the intelligent analytic process unfolds to add and rework each element. As you fill in the blanks look for the linkages—the connective tissue—between each element that, when completed, will deliver a strong lead paragraph that answers a known question for the audience. To start, answer the first three questions. These and the questions that follow are part of the preliminary work that needs to be done to draft the B.L.U.F.

What is your topic?

_____
_____
_____

Who is the audience?

_____

_____

_____

Why are you writing: what does the audience need from your assessment (context, background, support for a conference, board meeting presentation, or strategic planning)?

_____

_____

_____

Stop for now – you will come back to the remaining steps in the next chapters.

What is the KIQ?

_____

_____

_____

What data did you collect to answer the KIQ?

_____

_____

_____

How did you array the data?

_____

_____

_____

The title is a last of the three pieces. It summarizes the inference in 8–10 words and is explained and practiced in chapter 11.

A First Introduction to Inferences

While not formally part of the seven required elements the inference is a key element of the B.L.U.F. because it must lead the paragraph and in one sentence summarizes all its elements. It is so critical to conveying the message upfront that for the US intelligence services an inference must lead each written and oral assessment. For our purposes we define an inference as a logical conclusion that can be drawn from facts as known at the time of drafting and subject to change. In Intelligent Analysis this construct is critical because it anchors the look ahead in facts and as we will see it includes an estimated level of probability that a development or event will take place. Much more on this construct in chapters 6 and 7.

For now, to help visualize an inference, go back and reread the summary inference drawn above from the auto sales forecast. Then envision your target audience rushing to a meeting on auto sales projections and asking for a quick one sentence summary of your research. That quick response needs to be expressed in an inference to be helpful. Follow the example below that breaks down the inference in the sample B.L.U.F relating to auto sales projections into its component parts: A + B →C.

Fact A: The NADA PR head says tax cuts prevented a steeper decline in auto sales in 2018

+

Fact B: but with the bump gone, vehicle sales in 2019 will slip below 17 million vehicles for the first time in four years

→ **(implies): C** which very likely means dealers and manufacturers will continue to recalibrate production targets and incentives as continuing shifts toward SUVs and trucks and rising prices and interest rates prompt renewed focus on used cars.

Note how the (implied) → inference C is based on facts A and B. The level of probability, (very likely) reflects the level of certainty of the reporting. Much more on this as well.

B.L.U.F.: A Road Map for Drafting Longer Assessments

The B.L.U.F. paragraph provides a ready outline from which to build lengthier assessments. To start, go back and look at the B.L.U.F. template and see how each sentence can become an analytic paragraph lead. Figure 11 illustrates the process. Think of each B.L.U.F. element as a paragraph's analytic lead.

Here is an example of how it works, using an expanded version of the first three paragraphs of the auto sales article.

Title: Auto Industry Adjusting Incentives, Production Ahead of Anticipated 2019 Sales Decline

Inference: The NADA PR head says tax cuts prevented a steeper decline in auto sales in 2018, but with the bump gone vehicle sales in 2019 will slip below 17 million vehicles for the first time in four years, pushing dealers and manufacturers to recalibrate production targets and incentives as continuing shifts toward SUVs and trucks and rising prices and interest prompt renewed focus on used cars.

What's the new development driving the requirement?
NADA forecasts a decline in sales in 2019 and has convinced manufacturers to reduce production and available incentives to cut costs.
Use three data/reporting sources to answer the question above.

- Data/Reporting

- Data/Reporting

- Data/Reporting

Why is this development or event occurring now?
Our own review of the data confirms industry assessments that a combination of factors is impacting sales, including tariffs, trade negotiations, high interest rates, renewed focus on late model used cars, and shift to SUVs, trucks, and crossover vehicles.
List three points that answer the question above.

- _____

- _____

- _____

How is this happening?

Manufacturers have moved aggressively to protect profit margins including cutting production and largely shifting small car production to non-U.S. plants, and dealers have reduced buyer incentives.
List three points that answer the question above.

- ■ _____

- ■ _____

- ■ _____

What has been the impact of the development so far?

Reporting over the last three months indicates that manufacturers and dealers are already taking steps to mitigate the expected downturn.
Provide three points that answer the question above.

- ■ _____

- ■ _____

- ■ _____

Let's dissect how this sample B.L.U.F. was constructed.

The B.L.U.F. paragraph is broken out by sentence in the form of a question. For example, the first B.L.U.F. element, the "what," becomes:
What's the new development driving the requirement?

- ■ Supporting data/reporting
- ■ Supporting data/reporting
- ■ Supporting data/reporting

Then, the remaining B.L.U.F. elements follow the same approach.
Why is it happening now?

- ■ Supporting data/reporting
- ■ Supporting data/reporting
- ■ Supporting data/reporting

The Author's Rule of Thumb on Being "Stuck"

Key point: Working through the B.L.U.F. elements is hard work, and you may well find yourself stuck, that is, uncertain about whether you are on the right track. This challenge is especially common in drafting the inference. If you are stuck, don't be afraid to back off and start again. Try another approach to the B.L.U.F. rather than wrestle with language that will never work.

Here is my first real experience with "stuckness." I was at the time a very junior analyst. In the middle of a night shift during crisis coverage at CIA, it was my turn to do the overnight summary for senior readers, due at 5 a.m. I sat down at the typewriter (yes, a typewriter) and stared at the page. There were volumes of reporting, so much that I couldn't get started. I was stuck and just sat there looking at the paper. My shift manager stepped in and said he would do it and we would talk later. Here was his message over coffee slightly modified to tie it more closely to the book. If you are still staring at the screen trying to make your lead work after 10 minutes, it will never work. The lesson has stayed with me for 40 years and I pass it on in every class.

How does it work?

- Supporting data/reporting
- Supporting data/reporting
- Supporting data/reporting

And so on.

The end product is a skeleton outline. This approach makes writing longer assessments faster and easier. In fact, when this is done, drafting becomes a detail, not the usual agony. This approach to longer assessments:

- ***Separates the research and thinking from the drafting.*** These are three separate parts of the process and need to be done separately to maintain focus and avoid getting bogged down in crafting sentences.

■ *Limits supporting evidence to three data points:* Three makes your point. No need to use every shred of collected reporting in the text. Summary graphics can provide that extra detail.

■ *Makes the flow readily visible:* The skeleton outline gives you, your peers, and your supervisors a high-level view of the assessment that can reveal information gaps and shifts in focus away from the message.

■ *Facilitates collaboration:* To leverage expertise and speed up drafting, this format makes it easy to farm out specific sections and gives collaborators instructions about how to respond. It minimizes the surprises that come with incomplete or poorly crafted text.

Note: If the assessment has section headings or subtitles, they also need to align with the B.L.U.F. Subhead titles must be analytic. They capture the main point of the section in three to five words. This internal alignment will help busy readers to follow the story just by reading the assessment at any level, including just the title, the B.L.U.F. subheads, or just topic sentences. For example, the subsection on impact so far could be subtitled "Early Steps to Mitigate Losses."

Here are some last thoughts to close out this long chapter. More often than they may realize, analysts play a role in high stakes situations, and the B.L.U.F. is the analysts' most important vehicle to impact their organization's decisions. And good analysts want that impact. In this regard, the step-by-step process of crafting the B.L.U.F. requires analysts to bring their expertise and hard thinking to bear on each sentence in sequence, in order to tell their audience all they need to know the same way every time. The framework also discourages cutting corners because the paragraph quickly unravels if analysts skip or gloss over steps. This book's structure, and how the chapters build on each other, further reinforces the potentially serious consequences of lazy thinking.

There is no formal exercise as part of this segment, but an exercise is included as part of the blank assessment template in the appendix titled "Move Your Assessment Forward."

CHAPTER FIVE

Decision Maker Knowledge and Collaboration Shape Key Intelligence Question

> "If I had an hour to solve a problem and my life depended on the solution, I would spend the first 55 minutes determining the proper question to ask. For once I know the proper question, I could solve the problem in 5 minutes."
>
> —*Albert Einstein*

SUMMARY

Main Points

- Problem definition often stymies CEOs and analysts, prompting endless arguments about "What problem are we trying to fix." Getting it wrong can be catastrophic.

- In Intelligent Analysis, expertise combines with knowledge of, and collaboration with, the audience to formulate their KIQ(s), which represent their highest priority near- and longer-term issues.

- KIQs drive analysts' work: stories tracked, data collected, assessments written, and when. Answers are written in the B.L.U.F. format.

KIQs have fixed criteria:

- They must be open ended and allow for an answer with all B.L.U.F. elements. Yes or no questions are valid but often are about something broader.

- They must specify a time horizon. Does the question look at near- or longer-term priorities?

- They must avoid answering the question in the question. This can lead to selective data collection and a biased assessment.

- For decades, the US intelligence services have used a well-validated framework, known as the Intelligence Question Refinery, to craft KIQs.

- Sub-questions break down the KIQ and further refine it.

- Multiple examples and exercises facilitate practice in forming the KIQ for the analyst's project.

Key Takeaways

- Analysts find developing KIQs challenging because the questions are often too general, or because analysts assume they know audience requirements and what they need to hear. It is misleading to answer the question in the question.

- If analysts support multiple audiences, staying current is especially important because requirements will likely differ among them.

CHAPTER 5:
Decision Maker Knowledge and Collaboration Shape Key Intelligence Question

"If I had an hour to solve a problem and my life depended on the solution, I would spend the first 55 minutes determining the proper question to ask. For once I know the proper question, I could solve the problem in 5 minutes. The mere formulation of a problem is far more essential than its solution..."

—**Albert Einstein**

Goal: To be deliberate in combining deepened audience knowledge with substantive expertise to develop the right KIQ that targets the right issue at the right time to meet known near- and long-term requirements.

Objectives

At the end of this chapter, analysts will be better able to:

- Explain the significance of the KIQ.

- Understand the importance of collaborating with the audience to develop a precise KIQ.

- Identify the attributes of a good KIQ.

- Understand the risks of assuming that the audience is already known and answering the question in the question.

- Understand how to use the Intelligence Question Refinery framework to develop an agreed upon KIQ.

- Understand the value of sub-questions to further refine the KIQ.

- Develop a strong KIQ and sub-questions for your own project.

Answer the Right Questions at the Right Time

Knowledge of your audience and substantive expertise are two essential ingredients in formulating a timely KIQ (Walton, Intelligence Question Refinery; Walton, Presentation). The third ingredient is collaboration between analysts and their audience or their teams to make certain that the assessment answers the right question at the right time. Responding to this and other KIQs directs analysts' daily work, including what issues to track, what data to collect, and what is written and when. This also means that analysts need to be able to understand and respond to questions from multiple perspectives.

For example, new information arrives at your desk that you know would answer a senior decision maker's KIQ. At the same time, however, over the next half-hour, four different component heads send their own questions to you ahead of an upcoming meeting. The good news is that your outreach skills developed to build relationships with the audience(s) have paid off, but it's unclear from the questions they asked what they are really looking for or what they need, but you do know that a "one-size" answer will not fit all. There is work to do to clarify the requirements and sorting it out with stakeholders before drafting responses will help you avoid "firing blanks."

Good Key Intelligence Questions Meet Strict Criteria

In looking for clarity from each stakeholder, the analyst knows that, to be most helpful, the KIQs must:

- **Be open ended.** An open-ended question gives analysts the opportunity to provide a complete answer to the question with a complete B.L.U.F. This approach can help steer you and the audience away from simple yes or no answers. Note: yes or no questions are certainly valid and cannot be ignored, but generally the yes or no question is really about getting at something deeper. You need to ask for clarification: what does the audience really want to know?

  - For example, the audience wants a straightforward answer to this question: "Does this car run well?" Some follow-up questions, however, get at what the decision maker really wants to know: "What indications are there that this car

will satisfy my driving expectations?" The answer to the
first question is binary; the answer to the second question
requires a more comprehensive question.

- **Be time bounded.** They create a time frame (near- or longer-
term) and make room for context and trend lines.

   - For example, a question such as this—What indications
   are there that the airline will improve its on-time record?—
   provides no end of the story. Adding "over the next 30
   days" does the trick: it's a look at near-time possibilities.

- **Be audience approved up front.** Forming the question is a
collaborative process. Again, looking back at the questions
thrown at analysts, make sure that the question reflects what
was meant. Analysts generally feel inadequate going back to
the decision maker for clarification. But if you don't, you may
miss the mark and come up with the right answer to the wrong
question, resulting in eye rolls or "what's this?" and "thanks,
anyway, I needed it yesterday." Getting clarity about what is
really on their minds must be part of the process. It might be
called "peeling back the layers of the issue." It can take a while
but it's surprising, sometimes, that in the conversation the audience actually realizes they were asking the wrong question.
That's always a good moment.

- **Don't answer the question in the question.** This last standard
merits a deeper look because the serious consequences of vio-
lating this standard underscore the importance of getting the
question right. For example, look at these two questions:

   - Why is the bank involved in money laundering?

   - What makes this car manufacturer cheat on emissions
   tests?

Both questions are legitimate and based on indications of possible mal-
feasance. But a closer read shows that in both cases the questions assume
the bank and car manufacturer are guilty. Read them again. The answers are
predetermined. It's not that the bank and car manufacturer are not guilty, but

rather the questions pose a risk to analytic objectivity, which is so central to Intelligent Analysis. The questions' ripple effect begins with deciding what information to collect and ends with an assessment that is incomplete and likely biased. This failure of analytic tradecraft occurs when analysts believe they have enough information to convince themselves that their assessment is valid, and assume they know what the audience needs or wants to hear. They simply become locked in. Consider the impact of this assessment on an unknowing prosecutor deciding whether or not to issue indictments. And then consider another line of work.

EXERCISE: Turn These Questions into Good KIQs

Below are questions that clearly don't meet the criteria for a good KIQ. They are, however, questions that came to you from executives who expect a response.

Instructions:
Revise these questions to make them consistent with the criteria for a good KIQ. Refer back to the above examples as models.

Did you see this morning's WSJ headline? Holy cow!!

_____
_____
_____

Will Acme beat our new widget to market?

_____
_____
_____

Competition is everywhere: are we vulnerable?

_____
_____
_____

How is Acme doing these days?

_____

_____

_____

These second quarter numbers look ominous; where are we headed?

_____

_____

_____

How much business can we expect to do next quarter?

_____

_____

_____

Develop the Right KIQ: A Framework to Refine the Question

To help formulate a good KIQ that meets the criteria presented on pages 89-90, the US intelligence services for decades have used a well-validated framework that helps them be more deliberate in developing a KIQ that meets the audience's needs. The framework is called the Intelligence Question Refinery because it helps analysts be more deliberate in shaping a KIQ against a known decision maker requirement (Walton, Refinery). The framework might look straightforward, but it's often the analyst's most difficult challenge because it requires both expertise and audience knowledge and because of the ever present temptation to assume you know what they need. The refinery provides a process, but also works against answering the question in the question, which often involves getting rid of long-held habits. Most notably, the framework:

■ Drives a more deliberate process. By breaking down the KIQ into discrete parts it serves to counter the biases that can interfere with an assessment.

■ Broadens the response. Done right, the refinery drives the rest of the intelligent analytic process, especially what data to collect, which so often stymies analysts.

- Requires engagement with decision makers. With multiple decision makers focused on the same development with different questions, the refinery helps articulate the differences.

Figure 12 is a blank Intelligence Question Refinery followed by explanations for each column. An example of how a completed refinery might look draws on the article below on China's potential market for Chilean cherries. It provides a detailed example of how the refinery can help you shape the KIQ for multiple decision makers.

The five decision makers in the far left column are those that came to the analyst when the potential for entering market came to their attention. An exercise that focuses on your own project follows at the end of this chapter.

Before looking at the framework, stop here and read the article on the Chilean cherry industry that follows after Figure 12. Then, come back here to complete the template.

This template sets out the steps required to convert a raw analytical question into a refined one. The column titles are explained below.

1. Decision Maker	2. Development	3. Raw Question	4. Key Issue	5. Specific Decision Maker Interests	6. Time Frame	7. Refined Question
Director of marketing						
Strategic planning staff						
Chief scientist						
Chief logistics officer						
The CEO						

Figure 12. The Intelligence Question Refinery.

Explanation of columns:

The Decision Makers (Column 1): Listing them will help you see where the differences among them—in terms of what they want to know—start to appear.

Development (Column 2): Something just happened, and your decision makers are asking, "What does this mean?"

Raw Question (Column 3): This is an unrefined first reaction to the development: Is there anything to this report?

Key Issue (Column 4): What do you think is at the heart of the raw question? In the case presented in the article, based on the development, it's the potential for the cherry company to move into the Chinese market.

Specific Decision Maker's Interests (Column 5): What is this decision maker most concerned about currently? Each segment of the division might well have different concerns. This is where the question can become more tailored, but you need the decision maker's knowledge and input to refine the question.

Time Frame (Column 6): How far do you need to look ahead? What is the planning horizon? This could differ widely as well because of the multiple requirements that must be met.

Refined Question (Column 7): At last, prepare the refined question that meets the decision maker's requirement; make sure to review the question with the decision maker.

EXAMPLE AND EXERCISE:
Refinery Serves Multiple Decision Makers Focused on Same Development

Below is an example of a completed question refinery that can serve as a model that can be followed when drafting a KIQ for your project. Note that it shows how an analyst manages to develop refined questions for multiple stakeholders about the same development.

Perspective: You are a business intelligence analyst for a large US-based agricultural conglomerate with underutilized land in Chile. Decision makers from different departments ask if the company should consider entering the Chinese market. Their questions are vague (e.g., "What do you make of this report for our company?). Figure 13 illustrates the analyst's finished question refinery. You turn to the refinery on page 93 and, based on your chosen decision maker knowledge, formulate questions to guide the research for your assessment.

Instructions:

As you follow the example, note how the question evolves from a vague query to a targeted question that meets the criteria.

A Cheery Tale of Chilean Cherries
Government help and market forces create a new industry
The Economist, 17 January 2019

"I began to do cherries because it was difficult," says Hernán Garcés. The small, sweet fruit's easily damaged by rain, hail, or rough handling. They must be harvested by hand and processed individually. But the effort has paid off. Mr. Garcés, now known as the "father of Chilean cherries", has just guided the head of China's customs agency round his firm's plant, an hour's drive south of Santiago. Thanks to China's appetite for cherries, Garcés Fruit has become the world's biggest producer of them. Its output has increased 25-fold in 15 years. And Chile has a booming new industry. The mix of market forces and government help is an example of what Chile needs to escape from the "middle-income trap".

It's the country's good fortune that the southern-hemisphere cherry harvest comes just before Chinese New Year. Newly rich Chinese decisionmakers like to bestow on friends and family a gift of cherries, whose red, round form they see as symbolizing prosperity. Exported in elegant 5kg (11lb) boxes, the cherries are marketed as something closer to a luxury product than a humdrum fruit.

This means that quality is paramount. The cherries are pampered. At Greenex, a smaller firm, a $3.2m intelligent processing machine began work last month. It washes the fruit, then guides it into individual channels, where the stems are plucked out. The machine can sort by colour, form, weight and defects, explains Luis Dalidet, the young technician minding it. It discards around 15% of the fruit as inferior. That goes for sale in the local market. The machine will be used for only six weeks or so per year.

Seizing the opportunity of the Chinese market has required innovation. There are new varieties, and better farming practices such as high-density planting. Garcés Fruit uses giant fans to warm the trees in winter and, after heavy rains, draughts of air from a helicopter to dry the cherries, since damp can cause them to split. The biggest changes were in logistics. To pack his product Mr. Garcés brought plastic bags from the United States that regulate the air inside them (they are now made in Chile). Ships ply the route from Chile to China in 22 days, compared with 40 in the recent past.

Thanks mainly to Chinese demand, Chile exported $1.1bn-worth of cherries in 2018, double the value of 2017 and two-thirds that of its much better-known wine exports. Such is the potential demand in China that Mr. Garcés is confident that Chile's cherry exports can double again over the next five years.

That is welcome. If Chile is going to become a developed country, it must reduce its reliance on copper, which accounts for around half of its exports, and develop higher-value products. That transition be-gan in the 1990s, with rising exports of wine, salmon, and grapes, but had seemed to stall recently.

Creating new industries sometimes requires government in-volvement. The cherry industry would not exist but for Chile's free-trade agreement with China and its rigorous. sanitary standards, for example. Corfo, the state development agency, provides seed money for innovative ventures. It's inviting bids to build and run a centre to develop lithium batteries. The country also has potential in astrodata, according to Sebastián Sichel of Corfo. With its clear, dark skies, Chile's desert is home to several of the world's biggest telescopes. Astrono-my is the highest-paying profession in Chile, says Mr. Sichel.

But the cherry industry, and Chile's diversification, also owe much to market forces. Cherries require field labour, which Chileans spurn. Some 700,000 immigrants, mainly from Haiti and Venezuela, arrived between 2015 and 2017, averting a labour shortage. Farmers are tearing out vines to plant cherry orchards, which are more profitable. Farther south, apple growers are switching to hazelnuts for the same reason.

Peru has enjoyed a similar agro-industrial revolution. It rivals Chile in exports of blueberries. Competition is leading to specializa-tion. Peru and Chile squabble over trademark rights to pisco (a grappa named after a Peruvian seaport). Nevertheless, Chile is now importing Peruvian pisco, a superior product. Although the cheap local version remains the favourite tipple of hard-up young people, some Chilean pisco producers have switched to making good white wine. Had he lived to see this happy evidence of the invisible hand of market forces, Adam Smith might have downed a glass and polished off a bowl of cherries to celebrate.

This article appeared in the Americas section of the print edition under the headline "Adam Smith in Chile"

Figure 13 is a notional example of a completed refinery. Note how the data in each row shapes the refined questions to support each stakeholder.

Decision Maker	Development	Raw Question	Key Issue	Specific Decision Maker Interests	Time Frame	Refined Question
CEO	Report on Chilean cherry exports to China	Cherries, really?	What if we don't?	Where's the upside; what are the risks?	12-24 months	See below
Director of marketing	Report on Chilean cherry exports to China	Can we compete in China; where are other markets?	Is China market saturated; are there other markets?	How could we make ourselves competitive in a new market?	12-24 months	See below
Strategic planning staff	Report on Chilean cherry exports to China	Do cherries fit into our long-term planning?	What trade-offs would we have to make to do this?	Long-range implications of a new product line?	Five years	See below
Chief scientist	Report on Chilean cherry exports to China	What cherries, from where to where?	Where can they be acquired; can we grow them?	Can cherries be harvested and shipped to markets on time?	90 days	See below
Logistics/ shipping staff	Report on Chilean cherry exports to China	Can we ship them in a timely manner?	Do we have the capacity to ship?	What resources are needed to ensure safe, timely deliveries?	12-24 months	See below

Figure 13. Example of a completed Intelligence Question Refinery.

Here are some examples of what analysts' refined questions might look like pending audience approval.

- **CEO:** What indicators do we have that our company can become competitive in the cherry export market to China given Garcés's strength there?

- **Marketing director:** What indicators do we see that our company would be competitive in China's cherry market?

- **Strategic planning staff:** To what extent will entering the cherry market impact the company's long-term (five-year) plan for growth of its agro-industrial business?

- **Chief scientist:** To what extent are soil and moisture content on our farm capable of producing cherries that would be competitive in the China market?

- **Logistics/shipping staff:** To what degree is the company positioned to match established exporters' ability to reach emerging and new markets for cherries in a timely manner?

Note how these questions:

- **Remain open ended.** They don't lead to a predetermined answer and leave room for a full response. Use of terms such as to what extent, what factors, what indicators, or how well help in that regard because the response could be at any point along a continuum, depending on the reporting.

- **Reflect different perspectives among stakeholders.** One intelligence assessment cannot meet the needs of such different and important stakeholders. Note how much their questions differ in response to the same report, and how important the answers are to the company's decision.

- **Are tightly focused on the highest priority near-term issue.** Because developing the KIQ is a collaborative process, the analyst can distinguish the KIQ from the decision maker's other questions that may be important and need to be answered— but not now.

Sub-Questions Break Down Refined Questions

Widely recognized across disciplines, sub-questions break down refined questions to facilitate a still more focused response. Sub-questions are those that must be answered to respond to the KIQ. For an example, look at some possible sub-questions to break down the marketing director's refined question:

*"What indicators do we see that our company
would be competitive in China's cherry market?"*

Here are examples of possible sub-questions:

- What companies are currently in China or may be preparing to enter the market?

- To what extent is the cherry market saturated in China; does demand exceed supply?

- What distributors are there who can place our product in key markets?

- What are the fruit's characteristics that have made the Chilean companies successful?

The list could become long, even up to 15 or 20 sub-questions, but the analyst knows that while they are relevant to the broader question, only a few of them are needed to meet the decision maker's known immediate question. So, sub-questions serve several purposes:

- They quickly further narrow down the data search.

- Placed in the right order they can help structure the response.

- In a real time crunch they can be divided among colleagues to answer (but make sure they know how you want them answered—in a B.L.U.F. format).

- Sub-questions left unanswered can be the basis for follow-on pieces (with decision maker approval).

EXERCISE:
Develop the KIQ and Sub-Questions for Your Own Project

With the decision maker approved KIQ and sub-questions set, you are ready to do the research and prepare to answer the question(s). Remember that you may not be able to answer all the questions now without audience input. That's part of the exercise so don't guess.

Instructions:
Below is a blank refinery template for the exercise. Use it or duplicate it on paper or your computer.

Be deliberate and conscious of what your decision maker needs. Fill in each space that you can. Blank entries point out gaps in decision maker knowledge that need to be filled. Don't jump to the refined question. Getting this process right is key to the book's remaining exercises.

Draft a refined KIQ only for your chosen decision maker.

As reminders, explanations of the columns and the characteristics of a good KIQ are listed below the template. When you are done, compare your refined questions with the examples.

Decision Maker	Development	Raw Question	Key Issue	Specific Decision Maker Interests	Time Frame	Refined Question

Reminders

What Each Column Means

- Development: Something just happened, and your decision makers are asking, "What does this mean?"

- Raw Question: This is an unrefined first reaction to the development: Is there anything to this report?

- Key Issue: What do you think is at the heart of the raw question?

- Specific Decision Maker Interests: What is this specific decision maker most concerned about currently?

- Time Frame: How far do they need to look ahead? What is the planning horizon?

A good KIQ:

- Is open ended.

- Sets the time frame.

- Wins decision maker buy-in up front.

- Does not answer the question in the question.

Develop Sub-Questions

Instructions:
List five or six sub-questions that need to be answered to respond to answer your KIQ. After listing them, arrange them in an order that would help you structure your research and assessment.

_____

_____

_____

_____

_____

Getting the KIQ Right Really Matters

For Intelligent Analysis, the refinery accomplishes two important goals:

- It works against biases. Even experienced analysts, because they think they are so smart, are confident (overly so in some instances), or because they think they know the audience, may answer the question in the question. "Right, no question that the bank launders money," or "the cherry market in China looks like a sure bet." Such biases can cause even more harm if the question fuels the decision maker's predilections as well. Your mind will decide what data you select, how the B.L.U.F. is phrased, how you estimate probability, and on and on. If you find yourself unable to resist the temptation to please your audience look for something else to do with your life. You will fail as an analyst or, worse, do harm.

- It can kick-start an assessment. Developing the right KIQ combined with decision maker buy-in gives analysts the guidance to pull from that vast sea of information only the data needed to answer the decision maker's KIQ quickly and efficiently. That tsunami of information can now be run through a garden hose.

To close, in just these last two chapters you have identified your target audience, their requirements, and the KIQ that needs to be answered. Already that vast, intimidating pool of data has quickly become far more manageable. Now, you are ready to do the research to answer the question.

Before moving on, please go to the B.L.U.F. template on page 228 and enter your own KIQ. The linkage between the audience and requirements should be readily apparent.

CHAPTER SIX

Evidence-Based Decisions Mean First Collect, Count, and Array Data

"Without data, you're just another person with an opinion."

—*W. Edward Deming*

SUMMARY

Main Points

Intelligent Analysis is data driven and the data needs to be collected, arrayed, and analyzed first, because the answer is always in the data. Data is both digital and qualitative (from reports, articles, focus groups, surveys, and interviews).

- Knowing the audience and the KIQ sets sharp boundaries for what needs to be collected.

- Data serves three purposes: it creates a baseline (the "as is" state), points out changes in the baseline that need to be reported, and fuels assessments that feed into an organization's decision-making.

- On KIQs the threshold for reporting these changes (or not) is low—no more than one or two data points are required to inform the audience.

- Displays of data in charts, maps, and tables follow the same quality standards as written assessments.

Key Takeaways

■ This chapter emphasizes one essential point: the answer to the KIQ is in the changing (or static) trends and patterns that emerge from tables, charts, and graphs.

■ This means that the data must collected, arrayed, and analyzed first: that's the answer. The data speaks. Opinion has no place in Intelligent Analysis.

■ Printing out the KIQ(s) and keeping them in sight focuses the collection process. Data sources are endless, but only the facts that answer the KIQ matter.

The chapter has two related exercises involving (1) evaluation of graphics against quality standards and (2) identification of data sources and ideas for visuals for their assessment.

CHAPTER 6:
Evidence-Based Decisions Mean First Collect, Count, and Array Data

"Without data, you're just another person with an opinion."
—W. Edward Deming, Multiple Citations

Goal: To demonstrate an understanding that digital and qualitative data, clearly arrayed in charts, maps, and tables, is the starting point for producing evidence-based Intelligent Analysis that answers the audience's KIQ.

Objectives

At the end of this chapter, analysts will be better able to:

- Describe how decision maker knowledge and the right intelligence question significantly narrows down the scope of what needs to be collected from oceans of available information.

- Explain why Intelligent Analysis requires analysts to "count first."

- Explain the roles digital and qualitative data play in crafting evidence-based Intelligent Analysis.

- Explain why graphics and written intelligence assessments share the same analytic standards.

- Determine what types of data and graphics would best support your assessment.

Data Fuels Intelligent Analysis

Start with data, every time. With the KIQ approved, analysts head for the databases to pull out the information needed to answer the question with an evidence-based response. (This chapter draws on multiple sources: Davenport, 2013;" Pfreffer and Sutton, 2006; McKinsey;" Taleb, 2008, a, Taleb, 2008 b).

For the book's purposes, the term data is used to describe information found in two forms: quantitative and qualitative.

- *Digital* data is numeric. It measures values expressed as numbers (how many, how much, how often, where) arrayed in tables or charts.

- *Qualitative* data is less precise because it's non-numerical. It's information based on observations—data that can be observed and recorded—but also needs to be quantified to be useful. This type of data is collected, for example, through methods of observation: one-on-one interviews and focus groups as well as open-source reporting (print, other media), comments on survey forms, interviews, anecdotal observations, or official reports in hard or soft copy.

Data plays three essential roles in Intelligent Analysis.

1. Data creates a baseline (the "as is" state) for later comparisons when analysts first start looking at a problem.

2. Data points to changes in trends, patterns, and relationships that need to be reported.

3. Data fuels longer-term assessments that feed into decision-making.

The second point is especially important because it always raises the question of threshold: when to report a shift? Remember, analysts already have a baseline and have been tracking reporting against a known set of decision maker requirements and KIQs. A good rule to follow is that one or two data points is sufficient to warrant at least a heads-up. Here are some examples:

- First sign of an accounting problem ahead of a merger or acquisition or pension fund management.

- First anomaly in the performance of an aircraft or automobile.

- Early indications of the spread of a known gang from the southwest to the northwest part of the city.

- First signs of reputational damage in social media

In each instance it's up to the audience to decide what to do with the information. Your job is to inform. Be assertive. Holding back or waiting for one more piece of data can easily backfire. Your audience maker can always just set the information aside but may well also ask for more detail to avoid surprises.

Example of How It Works: Possible Shift in Criminal Activity

As an example of how data drives the analytic process, let's use both digital and qualitative data to take a deeper look into how an analyst tracks what *appears* to be a gang's spread from the southeast into the northwest part of the city. Figure 14 below illustrates how data drove the story.

The "as is" state identifies the level of activity before new reporting came in. It's the baseline. For example, on Friday when you went home the baseline was stable, but when you arrived on Monday, new reporting signaled a change from the baseline. In the case of possible shifts in criminal activity, the baseline had remained steady for several weeks in large part because of an expected seasonal slowdown as colder weather quieted the streets. The story shifted as limited data marked a change in the trend and pattern—criminal activity increased in the cold weather—that needed to be reported.

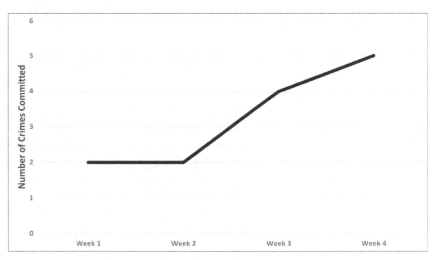

Figure 14. Criminal Activity in NW Quadrant, January 2020.

The increase in police-reported criminal activity attracts the attention of the analyst watching that neighborhood. The analyst, armed with his decision maker's known questions, deep expertise, and maps and charts, watches for more anomalies. Using quantitative data, the analyst has built a series of tables and maps that track what is known about the changes, including locations of current activity and possible gang involvement. The data shows the number of crimes committed held steady during the first two weeks of January, which is a typical pattern as winter starts to set in and street activity declines.

However, over the course of the last two weeks of January, police have provided qualitative reports from locals who observed an upturn in the of number of low-level crimes. Locals have also reported gang activity that included unknown teenagers, a rarity in a tightly knit neighborhood. Law enforcement has a good handle on the local players, but the fact that at least two of those arrested were new faces with new gang markings could indicate interlopers from across town or farther afield. The qualitative reporting marks another change in the pattern. The local police precinct asks the analyst for an update.

The analyst updates tables and maps with data from incoming crime reports, helping to confirm community residents' reports and law enforcement's own observations that points to possible shifts. The police step up collection and patrols to gather more data.

With the additional collection and more interviews and meetings with locals, the analyst turns to determining if the shifts are an anomaly or part of a more permanent change in gang dynamics that would increase the threat level to the northwest quadrant. During February, collection intensifies; the analyst pulls together the additional arrest data and any new gangs surfacing in the quadrant, and also asks the police to collect more observations from local residents. New graphics help the decision makers in law enforcement and city government to visualize numbers and "hot spots."

Finally, five weeks later the analyst produces a more in-depth assessment that includes a range of clearly arrayed data to help managers make resource allocation decisions and develop a plan to slow what now appears to be a real shift in that part of the city. The data tells an evidence-based story that helped law enforcement get ahead of the gang's activities.

Qualitative Data Needs to Be Quantified to Be useful

Note how the analyst and police used qualitative reporting to provide context. It reinforced digital data, provided a deeper look at the level of community concerns, and cataloged what residents had observed. These responses are called categorical data and are tabulated to quantify them and more readily integrate them into the analysis. The analyst tracking criminal activity in the city first made good use of quantitative data to spot and report the change and then added qualitative data to start to sort out the scope of the shifts in criminal activity. Over time this guided the stepped-up collection of information that provided stakeholders with the quantitative data needed to make resource allocation decisions.

Figure 15A summarizes the characteristics and utility of quantitative and qualitative data. Figure15B displays quantitative data. Figure 15C shows how qualitative survey data is quantified to be useful. It also shows how they can be combined to paint a more complete picture of the event or development.

	Quantitative	Qualitative
Goal	Discovering facts, explanation or causation	Learn what people are doing, and why they are doing it, from the participant's perspective; focus on meaning
Research Question	What, when, where and who questions	How and why questions; explanatory
Sample	Large number of people	Usually smaller groups of people
Data	Measurable data gathered via surveys or secondary data	Words, behaviors or visual; collected through participant observation or interviews to enhance understanding
Analysis	Statistical methods	Data analyze by themes, data is categorized into patterns

Figure 15A. Intelligent Analysis requires collection from both types of data source.

Another example:

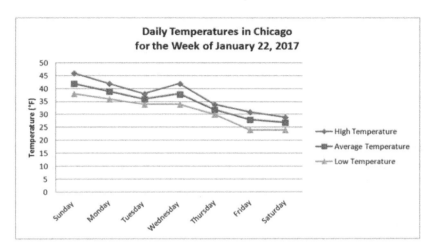

Figure 15B. Quantitative data tracks trends in temperatures in Chicago.

Figure15C. Qualitative and quantitative data combined tell a rich story.

Quality Standards Apply to Visuals

Data collection and visualization graphics are not an end in themselves. Rather, they are critical to helping you and your audience spot changes in trends, patterns, and relationships in stories you know your decision maker is following. And they will also help ensure that the analysis is derived from the data. For this reason, visuals and written intelligence assessments share the same analytic standards. Here is a summary of the graphics standards:

Visuals present one key point that jumps out at the viewer.

- Introductory language tells readers what they are seeing and ties it to the text.

- Visuals are placed near where their content is first discussed.

- Legends are easy to understand, and color schemes are clear and understandable to color-blind decision makers.

Visuals send a clear message.
They:

- Help to answer the decision maker's key intelligence question.

- Must be consistent with the text.

- Add or clarify information (context, background, data).

- Highlight or expand on aspects of the B.L.U.F.

Visuals present compelling reasons for accepting the graphic's significance.

- Visuals are well sourced and explain information gaps.

- Visuals don't play on emotions (e.g., photos or language are not used to generate sympathy).

EXERCISE:
Do These Graphics Meet Intelligence Quality Standards?

The open literature includes literally thousands of graphics that can be evaluated as to how well they track with the criteria. Figures16, 17 and 18 will get you started. See if you can write a sentence that captures their meaning. If not, why not?

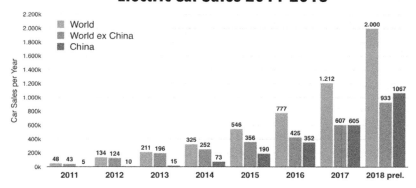

Note: Only BEV and PHEV cars; excluding trucks and buses. Source: Global Energy Briefing No.171 Jan19

Figure 16. Electric Car Sales, 2011-2018

What are the graphic's strengths?

_____

What areas need improvement?

_____

Write a sentence that conveys the graphic's message.

Top 10 BEV Markets by Volume H1 2019	Sales (k)	Δ 18 vs 19
1 China	430.7	+111%
2 USA	116.2	+87%
3 Norway	36.3	+74%
4 Germany	33.0	+72%
5 France	24.3	+38%
6 Netherlands	17.8	+118%
7 Korea	17.7	+63%
8 Canada	13.1	+37%
9 UK	12.7	+62%
10 Japan	11.0	-27%

≥JATO

Figure 17: Global Sales of Pure Electric Cars, 2018 vs. 2019 (JATO).

What are the graphic's strengths?

_____

What areas need improvement?

_____

Write a sentence that conveys the graphic's message.

For brands they are loyal to, consumers are willing to:

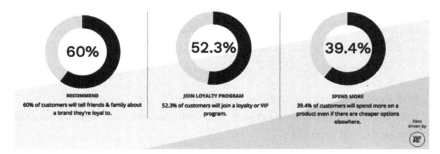

Figure 18. Yotpo Survey from Marketing Land, September 2019.

What are the graphic's strengths?

_____

What areas need improvement?

_____

Write a sentence that conveys the graphic's message.

EXERCISE:
Collect and Array Data for Your Own Assessment

The following exercise will help you focus on data collection and think about how it can be arrayed to help you and your decision maker visualize its significance.

Preparation: Recall your target audience.

_____
_____
_____

Make sure the KIQ is readily visible.

_____
_____
_____

What type of assessment is needed (context, explanation, trend assessment, warning, etc.)?

_____

_____

_____

With this information in hand, decide:
What digital data would you collect to meet your decision maker's requirement; where is it located?

_____

_____

_____

What qualitative data would you collect to answer the question; where is it located?

_____

_____

_____

List specific ideas for how you would array the data: maps, tables, charts. A description and/or sketch would be fine. Recall that the intent is to allow you to see what's in the data and then help your audience see what's not in the data in the form of an inference (expanded on in the next chapter).

_____

_____

_____

CHAPTER SEVEN

Arrayed Data Answers Key Intelligence Question Through Inferences

"Numbers have an important story to tell. They rely on you to give them a clear and convincing voice."

—Stephen Few, *Perceptual Edge*

SUMMARY

Main Points

- An inference is derived from analysis of the data collected and arrayed. It is defined as the logical conclusion from facts known or assumed to be true at the time they are expressed and *must be subject to change with new information.*

- In one sentence the inference summarizes the B.L.U.F.'s answer to the audience's KIQ. It includes key facts (as known then), implications for their organizations, and an estimated probability (highly likely, likely, probably, unlikely) that the event or development will occur. It is not easy to craft but may be all that busy readers have time to absorb.

- The title (explained in chapter 11) then summarizes the inference in 10 words or less.

- Here is how the inference is constructed in the example contained in the chapter:

  A *(fact as known)* + **B** *(fact as known)* → **C** *(the inference/conclusion)*

  "what" + *"what" implies "so what"*

  (A) The roads are clear + (B) the car runs well, so Tom (→ C) *will likely* arrive on time.

- This inference says that the data is good, which implies (sets the expectation of) when Tom will arrive. If new data shows changes, Tom will still get home, but the probability ("will likely") needs to express less certainty. So, the new data weakens the assumptions that underpin what can be concluded or inferred from the data, which must then change.

- To be clear: what can be inferred or concluded from facts A + B depends on the data that supports the assumptions. Think of it as an algorithm:

- Data → Assumptions → Inferences.

Key Takeaways

- This relationship links the audience, the KIQ, and the arrayed data to answer the question.

- The chapter includes multiple examples and two exercises. The first is to practice developing an inference and the second, to develop an inference for the project selected by each analyst based on their work so far.

CHAPTER 7:
Arrayed Data Answers Key Intelligence Question Through Inferences

"Numbers have an important story to tell. They rely on you to give them a clear and convincing voice."

—**Stephen Few, Perceptual Edges**

Goal: To understand how inferences drawn from collected and arrayed data reveal shifts in trends, patterns, or relationships and become the basis for the response to the KIQ that includes estimates of the probability that the event or development will occur.

Objectives

At the end of this chapter, analysts will be better able to:

- Describe the relationship between inferences, assumptions, and data in Intelligent Analysis.

- Explain why inferences are structured using the formulation $A + B \rightarrow C$.

- Describe how inferences express the probability of the relationship between facts as known and a look ahead that answers the decision maker's question.

- Make a (very tentative) first draft of an inference based on your own assessment using the structure $A + B \rightarrow C$, which draws on the data collected and arrayed to answer your decision maker's KIQ. Subsequent chapters will assist you in refining the draft.

NOTE: This chapter includes multiple terms that may be unfamiliar, especially those around the most likely outcome and estimating and expressing levels of estimated probability. Don't be concerned. These will be explained here and in depth in subsequent chapters and revised along the way. For now, focus on the purpose of inferences and how they are formulated.

Data-Driven Inferences Lead B.L.U.F.,
Summarize Response to Audience's KIQ

In Intelligent Analysis an inference always leads the B.L.U.F. paragraph. For senior executives inferences answer their KIQ in one sentence. It explains the implied relationship between what's known from collected data about the development or event. It also expresses the most likely outcome, which includes an estimate of the probability that the event or development will likely occur, and its implications. Think of it as the "so what" for the audience. The B.L.U.F.'s seven elements follow in their complete form, providing the audience with more detail. Underscoring their importance in meeting their audiences' requirements for a summary answer to the KIQ, the US intelligence services are required to start every written assessment and oral presentation with an inference. (ICD, 203; Taleb, 2008a, Taleb b)

In this book, inferences are defined as logical conclusions from facts known or assumed to be true at the time they are expressed, and which are subject to change. Specifically, new developments or events are expressed as changes (or not) in trends, patterns, or relationships. The concept may be more familiar as the "if . . then" formulation subject to the same rules. Here is the construct the book will use to help you craft an inference that answers the KIQ.

A (fact as known) + **B** (fact as known) → **C** (the inference/conclusion)
"what" + "what" implies "so what"

- A and B are the facts as known at the time that emerge from the tables, charts, or maps created to answer the decision maker's KIQ (and are subject to change).

- The arrow (→) is a recognized sign used here to imply a relationship between the "what" (facts) and the "so what" (C) that can be inferred at that time and that answers the KIQ based on facts known at the time.

- The arrow (→) is a symbol for language that conveys the strength of that implied relationship as an estimate of probability (probably, likely, unlikely, etc.) that the event or development will take place (subject to change or not with new information).

**Data Quality Determines Assumptions' Validity,
Inference's Estimated Probability**

These expressions of probability are called caveats because they signal or
warn the audience of the strength of the relationship between the facts and
what can be inferred from those facts. Note the difference between these two
inferences:

- The company's track record is solid and the market for its products is strong, which *probably* makes it good a target for acquisition.

- The company's track record is solid and the market for its products is strong, which is *highly likely* to make it a good target for
  acquisition.

The facts are the same in both inferences, but the analysts applied different caveats to describe the relationship between the facts and what can be
inferred from the facts, which would result in very different responses to the to
the audience's KIQ. More on this later. What follows is an example to help clarify
the relationship between the inference and the data.

1. Inference: Conclusions drawn from what we believe to be known facts.
The algorithm looks like this:

A (fact as known) + B (fact as known)]→C (what can be inferred/con-
cluded)
"what" "what" implies the "so what"

- For example, the road is clear, and the weather is good, so I will
  be home in an hour.

2. Assumptions: Conditions that *must* persist for an assessment to remain
valid at the stated level of certainty as caveated (and expressed with words
such as *will, probably, likely, about even, unlikely, remote/highly unlikely, could,
might, may, should,* and *would*).

- For the estimated driving time of 60 minutes to hold at such a
  high level of certainty ("I *will* be home") the driver assumes the
  roads and weather will remain clear throughout the trip.

- Another driver, however, is more cautious and looking at the data at departure is less certain that the assumptions will hold and concludes that the driving time *probably* will be 60 minutes.

3. Data: Qualitative and digital data described in the last chapter underpin the assumptions' validity. Both drivers in the example assessed the data to make their initial assumptions and the likelihood that they would hold up for the entire trip. Their level of certainty differed ("will" vs. "probably will") because of how they interpreted the data that underpins their assessment.

A look back at the Chilean cherry article where the analyst responds to the chief scientist's sub-question about the climate of the proposed growing areas provides a more realistic illustration of the relationship between the level of certainty expressed in the inference and data. Here is the analyst's response:

"According to reliable temperature tracking data bases, the week-long freeze reported in Chile's cherry-growing region is the fourth and longest over the last six years, which will very likely require a deeper look into the growing region's long-term viability to support such extensive exports."

Here are the judgments set out in the A + B → C framework:

A (Fact as known): "According to reliable temperature tracking data bases,"

+

B (Fact as known): "the week-long freeze reported in Chile's cherry-growing region is the fourth and longest over the last six years,"

→ implies a relationship between the two facts, which tells the scientist that

C: the company *probably will need* to take a deeper look into the long-term viability of the proposed growing region to support such extensive exports.

Note that the data supports the assumptions that underpin the inference that directly answers the scientist's KIQ. While it's only the analyst's first look

at one issue related to the region's potential to support large-scale cherry orchards, there is still enough information to provide at least a preliminary report
to the scientist that the increasing frequency and length of the freezes raises
the risk level to a point that warrants additional research.

Let's look at a very real example of the relationship between facts, assumptions, and inferences using a study which a community group in Chicago
undertook to produce a data-driven assessment of the possible linkages between poverty and drug-related arrests. Figure 19 displays the results.

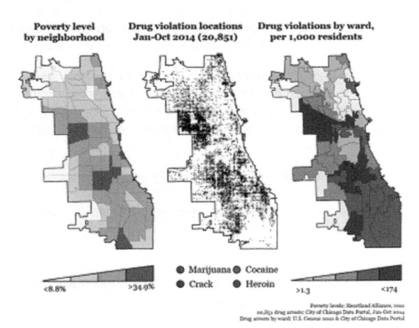

Figure 19. Scattergram correlating poverty by neighborhood with incidents of drug
violations in 2011 (source: Heartland Alliance).

While the scatter plot is too dense to sort out specific locations by drug and
neighborhood, a quick glance across the maps looking left to right provides
an overall picture that points to a possible correlation—if not yet causation—
between poverty levels, drug violations, and the impact of law enforcement
in the same neighborhoods per 1,000 residents. This relationship can be ex-

pressed as an inference that captures what is known and the level of certainty in what it shows. It's the "so what" for the decision maker. For example:

A (Fact as known): Data collected from all three maps in Figure 22 between 2011 and 2014

   +

B (Fact as known): and qualitative data from hundreds of interviews illustrating a possible correlation between residents' location, economic status, drug use, and arrests for drug violations,

   → implies a relationship between the two facts and the inference

C: that *likely* will require more detailed data analysis to determine if poverty is the primary cause of the high rate of drug use and arrests in the city.

Community leaders did not win funding in their meeting but were at least able to use the data to make their point—the "so what" for the target audience—to the city. But correlation is not causation, so while scatter plots are informative from a high-level perspective, city officials would want to look more deeply into the relationship to confirm the linkages and then target resources more effectively. The meeting was a good start because the appeal was evidence based with data and arrayed in a way that could be understood. While community leaders could have argued their point using just qualitative data, the number of questions it would have raised with officials would have sent it right to a committee to—that's right—request more specific data.

Be Careful of Drawing Inferences from Inferences

Making a follow-on inference from an implied relationship between facts raises risks of generating misleading conclusions. The construct of an inference drawn from an inference would look like this:

$$A + B \rightarrow C \rightarrow D$$

This formulation tells your audience that the implied relationship between the facts and C can be the basis for inferring D. But is inferring D always a risk? The answer is, of course, it depends. D is an inference drawn from an inference, that can either enhance the inference or mislead your decision maker. For example, look at this straightforward inference that works:

A: The jet stream has dropped from Canada into the Midwest

+

B: and moisture is coming from the south

→ implies the relationship between the facts (A and B) and the inference that the probability of the event occurring is "likely"

C: of snow or sleet over the next 24 hours.

Let's return to the weather forecast with *D* added:

It would be safe to say:

A: The jet stream has dropped from Canada into the Midwest

+

B: and moisture is coming from the south

→ implies that the two fronts together increase the likelihood (the estimated probability)

C: of snow or sleet over the next 24 hours

+

D: that in the past have shown the potential to quickly morph into dangerous blizzards accompanied by widespread power outages and unsafe traveling conditions.

In this instance, *D* is a data-based inference drawn from past weather patterns, so it's rooted in data and flows logically from *C*.

Now look at this example where D is incorrectly inferred from C:

A: The jet stream has dropped from Canada into the Midwest

+

B: and moisture is coming from the south,

→ which likely increases the chances

C: of snow or sleet over the next 24 hours,

+

D: which portends a major blizzard that will result in widespread deaths and power outages.

The warning expressed in *D* may well be true, but unless there is a well-validated track record of such extensive weather-related losses, it's not based on the meteorologist's current or past information. Without those roots in reporting, it's just an unwarranted warning based on an opinion that exaggerates the risk.

One more (safe) example is perhaps closer to home.

A: The house is well priced

   +

B: and meets all our criteria for size and location,

     → which implies that the house would likely

C: be a good purchase for us

     → that is unlikely

D: to require major repairs.

Clearly, *D* cannot be inferred from *C*. For *D* to be true at that level of probability would require substantially more information, perhaps in the form of a home inspection to validate the buyers' impressions of the home's condition and an escrow account to hedge against unseen problems. Otherwise, D becomes a prediction, and who wants to buy a house on hopes, dreams, and luck.

Let's finish this chapter with a practice exercise.

EXERCISE:
Answer the Investor's Question with an Inference

Below is a short article on the potential for developing a vaccine against typhoid fever.

Perspective: Your senior decision maker is an investor looking for an assessment of what pharmaceuticals offer the best opportunities for growth.

Key Intelligence Question: To what extent would an investment in the typhoid vaccine benefit shareholders?

INSTRUCTIONS

Read the article below on typhoid vaccine and develop an inference from the data that answers the intelligence question using the formulation A + B →C.

Remember the information can answer multiple questions for multiple decision makers, but you are interested *only* in answering the investor's question. If you find yourself thinking of the importance of good public health outcomes as a good investment, your heart is in the right place, but the audience will wonder what happened to the KIQ. Avoiding the trap of drifting away from the KIQ can be challenging, and it happens a lot.

Public Health: A Newly Revived Vaccine May Deal a Death Blow to Typhoid Fever
It languished for 20 years for lack of development money
The Economist, February 2, 2019

A BACTERIUM called Salmonella typhi travels from host to host in contaminated food and water. Thanks to better mains and drains its excursions have been curtailed in rich countries. But the disease that it causes—typhoid fever—is still common in places where modernity has not fully made its mark. In these parts between 11m and 20m people fall ill with typhoid every year. Of those 160,000, mostly children, die.

Typhoid fever can be treated with antibiotics, but this line of defence is starting to fail as extensively drug resistant (XDR) bacteria are spreading rapidly and alarmingly in Pakistan. Existing vaccines provide only temporary protection to adults and don't work in children. What is needed is a new and better vaccine. And one is now at hand, courtesy of the Bill and Melinda Gates Foundation, a big charity.

The origins of this vaccine, which labours under the moniker of Typbar-TCV, can be traced back to work done 20 years ago by researchers at America's National Institutes of Health. It was only ever licensed to Bharat Biotech, based in Hyderabad, India, for local use. Nobody else thought it worthwhile developing. Now the Gates Foundation has plucked Typbar-TCV from obscurity and pushed it through the research and testing necessary for it to be used everywhere.

One of the first of those tests was conducted by the Oxford Vaccine Group (OVG), a research organisation in Britain, in 2017. Andrew Pollard, OVG's boss, recruited 100 adult volunteers, vaccinated them, and then gave them a drink laced with live S. typhi. Britain was a good place to do this because typhoid is essentially extinct there, so participants had no existing immunity. Antibiotics were on hand to treat those who succumbed, but most did not. This and subsequent experiments have shown the vaccine to be almost 90% effective and, crucially, safe for use in children as young as six months.

Fever pitch

The Gates Foundation has just sent a supply of 200,000 doses of Typbar-TCV to Pakistan, to try and fight the outbreak of XDR typhoid there. In Sindh province (mostly in the capital, Karachi), there were 5,274 cases of XDR typhoid (of 8,188 cases overall) between November 1st, 2016 and December 9th last year.

The new vaccine has also been warmly welcomed by GAVI, an international health organisation formerly known as the Global Alliance for Vaccines and Immunisation, which has promised to spend $85m on Typbar-TCV this year and next. GAVI was supposed to start vaccinations in Zimbabwe this week. The doses are already in the country. However, according to Seth Berkley, GAVI's boss, strikes, protests and a deteriorating security situation have meant that the beginning of the campaign has been postponed until February 23rd.

Other places where the vaccine could be deployed include Bangladesh, Ghana, India, Nepal, Nigeria and Uganda. Besides being able to bring typhoid outbreaks in countries like these to a halt, vaccination may also help drive down the use of antibiotics, and thus, the selection pressure that maintains XDR bacteria in the population. Anita Zaidi, head of the vaccine-development, surveillance, and enteric and diarrhoeal diseases programmes at the Gates Foundation, even wonders if it might be possible to eliminate typhoid entirely if enough people are vaccinated.

That is an aspiration. Typbar-TCV does, though, bring the immediate hope of saving many lives. What a shame it has arrived 20 years later than it might have done.

Now summarize the article based on the A + B → C formulation.

A:

_____

_____(known fact)

+

B:

_____

_____(known fact)

→ _____ (level of probability)

C: _____

_____

EXERCISE:
Summarize Your Own Work So Far

We want to stop here and pull together the results of the exercises completed so far to make sure we are still on track. This exercise starts with several questions from the first four chapters. It then asks you to complete the first four elements of the B.L.U.F. template that focus on what is known based on the data which you collected and arrayed. From here we shift from what's known to what's ahead. The goal here is to help you see the "connective tissue" between the different elements of the intelligent analytic process that underpin the B.L.U.F. More follows.

- Make sure you have done enough research to complete the questions.

- You have already done the initial hard thinking. So, use what you have done on your worksheets but know that you will make multiple changes along the way, so don't worry.

- Once filled in, convert the responses into a paragraph and check for alignment.

INSTRUCTIONS:
Answer the following questions drawn from the template that is included below as a reminder.

What topic are you working on?

_____

_____

What is your working title? (8-10 words) We will come back to this when it is
Discussed in depth in chapter 11

_____

_____

Who is the audience for your assessment? (senior executive decision maker)

_____

_____

What is the purpose of your assessment for this audience? (inform, warn,
target, allocate resources)

_____

_____

What is your audience's KIQ?

_____

_____

What data did/will you collect to answer the question? (Make sure you have
done enough research.)

_____

_____

How do you plan to array the data?

_____

_____

Now complete the B.L.U.F. elements below. Answer in full sentences. Right,
some of this may seem repetitious. You will enter them into the B.L.U.F. tem-

plate later. Recall that this is just a draft and will be refined as you work through the chapters.

What is the development that made you write? (Recent reporting indicates, suggests, points to a new trend, pattern, relationship.)

_____

_____

Why are you writing now? (This matters now because . . .)

_____

_____

How does it work? (Important but optional: Is there a process or narrative sequence that decision makers need to know about to understand your assessment?)

_____

_____

What has been the impact of the development so far? (What does the data show? It may be that there is not information to point to any impact at this point.)

_____

_____

Based on your responses, write down the very first draft of the lead inference. You will use it in the next three chapters. It's only a draft.

_____

_____

CHAPTER EIGHT

A Deeper Look at Assumptions and Data Quality Sharpen Probability Estimates

"Probability is the measure of the likelihood that an event will occur."

—Nasim Taleb, *Fooled by Randomness*

SUMMARY

Main Points

- With this chapter we build on the introduction to inferences in the last chapter and shift from B.L.U.F.'s first four elements that set out what's known to the last three that focus on developing the most likely outcome—the "so what" and its implications for the audience, the "so what of the so what." To make the transition we revisit Tom's commute with the additional participation of his brother and mother to see how he assessed that he "will likely" be home on time and how new data changes that assessment. The first measure is the data's level of certainty (how strongly it supports the implied level of certainty); and the second, the level of confidence in the data (the source's reliability).

- In brief, the quality of the information collected, arrayed, and analyzed at the time of drafting determines the estimated level of probability that the event or development expressed in the inference will occur.

- US intelligence services use an agreed-upon vocabulary to express levels of probability.

- Ignoring new information that changes the estimate undermines decision-making and puts the audience and organization at risk; *it is the second cardinal sin after answering the question in the question in the KIQ exercise.*

Key Takeaways

■ Estimating probability is not guessing, but rather the careful evaluation of the implied (→) relationship between facts and the probability that the event or development will occur.

■ The audience almost always overestimates the ability of analysts to provide precise assessments of what is ahead, but analysts can only provide a range of possible outcomes with assigned estimates of probability.

■ Analysts must not succumb to pressure to go beyond the reporting and drift into opinions or "hazard a guess." It comes to no good. Always tie the look ahead to reporting.

■ The chapter provides detailed explanations and examples and introduces the vocabulary of probability; exercises reinforce the importance of developing clearly articulated assumptions.

■ As an exercise, the Source Assessment Framework provides a guide to developing a level of confidence statement.

CHAPTER 8:
A Deeper Look at Assumptions and Data Quality
Sharpen Probability Estimates

"Probability is the measure of the likelihood that an event will occur."

"Probability is not about the odds, but about the belief in the existence of an alternative outcome, cause, or motive."

—**Nassim Taleb,** *Fooled by Randomness*

Goal: To understand that the estimated level of probability of the event or development occurring which is expressed in the inference that leads your B.L.U.F. depends on the level of certainty and the reliability of the information that supports the inference's underlying assumptions

---

Objectives

At the end of this chapter, analysts will be better able to:

■ Explain the central role that clearly articulated assumptions play in estimating probability.

■ Distinguish between working, key, and linchpin assumptions.

■ Avoid common mistakes in managing assumptions that raise the risks of misleading your audience.

■ Explain how the measure of the level of confidence (reliability) in your data, which differs from the level of certainty, impacts the estimate of probability.

■ Use the Source Assessment Framework to help determine the level of confidence.

Estimating the Probability of Outcomes Hinges on Assumptions' Validity

The validity of an assumption—how well the facts support it—determines how analysts characterize the estimated level of probability (likely, unlikely, will…) that an event or development will occur (A + B → C). For the audience, the facts and the inference's implied (→) level of certainty is the answer to the KIQ and its implications for the organization. This assessment is the heart of Intelligent Analysis. It's every decision maker's key demand and analysts' biggest challenge. It's why analysts are so important, and it's what the audience needs most from you to transform known facts into evidence-based actionable intelligence.

Providing that balanced, data-driven look-ahead, however, remains the most challenging stage of Intelligent Analysis. Analysts can only estimate the probability of a range of possible outcomes, while the audience, especially if unfamiliar with intelligence analysis, often harbors unrealistic expectations of certainty and sees terms such as *likely, probably,* or *unlikely* lacking the certainty they are looking for to make decisions. They will push analysts to provide more precision, which can draw them into punditry, or to hazard an opinion about a hypothetical outcome. For example, being asked to give your best guess or opinion invariably leads to more speculation as you drift further from the reporting. Especially new, but even experienced, analysts looking for relevancy or to be helpful can easily find themselves crossing that line and providing a response with a false sense of precision and then taking the blame for what is likely a "bad call." Getting it right is just luck.

Unconsciously or not, audiences pressure analysts for an assessment of how closely the evidence supporting the assumptions comes to making the implied inference a fact. For example, based on facts A + B, a company's continuing success implies that its long-term success is a certainty/highly likely. The choice of caveat signals to the audience how closely the company's success comes to being a fact, or a certainty. In developing actionable intelligence each of these characterizations—explained earlier as caveats-- signals a different sense of assurance to the audience (A + B → C). The US intelligence services have used these caveats for decades to express estimated probability. Deciding on that caveat, however, is not guesswork but rather the end product of a rigorous process that is broken down in each of the book's remaining chapters, showing how assumptions become the basis for shaping the B.L.U.F.'s last three elements and starting with the most likely outcome.

Fixed Process Selects Working, Key, and Linchpin Assumptions

Shifting from what's known to what's next begins with deciding which assumptions—conditions that must persist—matter most to the inference's estimated probability. This book uses the US intelligence services' approach. The strength of the process is in the structured discussion among stakeholders that's intended to minimize the impact of biases and emotions and keep the process focused on the evidence. While the process is best done with relevant stakeholders, if necessary it can also be accomplished on your own or with a partner. Here are the steps using the outlook for a community bank's future as an example.

1. ***Develop working assumptions.*** Make a list of all the possible conditions that must persist to support the estimated probability. The list should include all the assumptions that could plausibly matter. It can be lengthy but should generally consist of no more than 20. Be sure to make them positive statements because you want to decide what conditions must persist rather than conditions that must not persist, which could number in the hundreds. For example, "wages remain steady" rather than "wages don't fall." This is a small but crucial difference; they must be conditions that need to persist. Here are some possible working assumptions related to the bank:

- The current management remains in place for the next three years.

- The loan portfolio remains free of sub-standard loans.

- The bank has a succession plan in place to ensure leadership continuity.

- The community remains economically healthy.

- The bank develops new services to offer.

- The bank sustains its high reserves.

- The bank stays in compliance with all regulations.

- Local competition remains at current levels.

The list could go on.

2. ***Identify the key assumptions.*** From the list of working assumptions, select no more than five or six assumptions that are the most important conditions that must hold in order to support the inference's estimated level of probability.

- The bank sustains its high reserves.

- The bank stays in compliance with all regulations.

- Local competition remains at current levels.

- The current management remains in place for the next three years.

- The community remains economically healthy.

3. ***Select linchpin assumptions*** These one or two assumptions are selected from the key assumptions. They are called linchpins because of their preeminent importance in supporting the inferences' estimated level of probability. Linchpins are discussed in much more depth in chapters 9 and 10, when we revisit the Key Assumptions Check (KAC) mentioned in chapter 1. The KAC systematically tests the validity of the assumptions in a process that helps you sort out how to characterize the relationship between the facts as known and what can be inferred from them (likely/highly likely, probably). For illustrative purposes, however, assume that the linchpins listed below flowed from the KAC results.

- The community remains economically healthy.

- The current management remains in place for the next three years. (Process drawn from Davis,1997; Heuer, 1999; Taleb, 2008a; Taleb, b)

Differences among Analysts Are Always about Assumptions

When analysts argue about what caveat best characterizes the relationship between the facts and what can be inferred from the facts, they are unconsciously or (less likely) consciously differing over which assumptions are key and linchpin and about the strength of evidence that supports each one.

This hypothetical scenario about two brothers commuting home illustrates what drives the differences and how they impact probability.

- Tom calls his mother from the highway and says, "I am on the road now. Traffic looks good *so I infer that I will be* home in 30 minutes."

- Bob calls his mother along the same route and says, "I am on the road now. Traffic at this point looks OK, *so I infer that I will probably* be home in 30 minutes."

- Mom thinks: Both my sons have started out with the same information and the same route, but Tom expresses a higher level of certainty in his inference ("will") than Bob, who is more cautious ("probably"). I don't know what to expect. I will check with them about how they estimated their arrival time when they eventually get here (Mom has read this book).

- Tom arrives around the same time Bob shows up, which is well beyond Tom's estimate. Mom asks Tom why he was so confident about a 30-minute drive time given the potential for delays. Basically, she is asking him why he characterized the inference as a fact ("will") based on the data available to support his assumptions.

- Tom reflects on the question and says that he made six assumptions. In no particular order, they are:

  1. Traffic patterns remain the same.

  2. The weather remains clear.

  3. The car remains mechanically sound.

  4. The roads are accident free.

  5. Information on road conditions is reliable.

  6. The car has sufficient fuel and snacks.

He goes on to say that the linchpins were assumptions 4 and 5 and, based on the data he had at the start of his trip, he estimated he would have a trouble-free journey.

- Mom says, "But this was not case."

- Tom says, "Right. Looking back, those two linchpin assumptions that were most critical for the high level of certainty unraveled pretty quickly. Two accidents occurred and my reliance on traffic updates on the radio proved mistaken. I should have updated my inference based on the new data. Better still I might have been more cautious in my assessment."

Let's assume (again, hypothetically) that Bob had the same list of assumptions and selected the same linchpins. Without more evidence that they were well supported, however, he was more cautious ("probably") in his estimate of how close his assumptions came to being facts. Mom is happy.

The story's outcome raises two critical points about the relationship between assumptions and the implied strength of what is inferred; specifically, how close the inference is to being a fact.

- First, even though the estimated probability of Bob's and Tom's inferences had different outcomes, the inference remained valid because the inference held up—they got home--*but at differing levels of probability* because the brothers had different assessments of the data's validity. Tom made a risky, straight line estimate. He was counting on the data he gathered at the outset of his trip to support his assumptions for the entire journey. For him, the likelihood of his assumptions holding made his inference a near fact. In contrast, Bob was more cautious and used "probably" to describe how closely the assumptions made the inference a fact.

- Second, the argument about how close the inference was to being a fact was about how they each evaluated the data. For Tom, it (1) clearly supported his assumptions; and (2) the data came from historically reliable media sources. Bob had that same information but did not agree that the data at the outset would remain static for the entire trip; he had been fooled too many times to warrant making the inference a fact ("will"). That is, Bob was less certain the assumptions would remain valid given the unpredictability and likelihood of new data coming in that would impact his estimated travel time. So, he opted to used "probably" to caveat his inference, leaving room for another outcome.

Again, for emphasis here is the most critical point: the inference was still valid—each brother would get home—but at different levels of estimated probability. Specifically, each brother evaluated the validity of the same assumption differently. This dynamic surfaces frequently in meetings where the stakeholders are arguing or at least seem to be talking past each other. At that point, it might be useful to slow everyone down and start to ask about their assumptions to break the log jam, even if they don't want to. Indeed, one important upside of the Tom and Bob episode was that both clearly articulated their assumptions. Their discussion gave Mom and each brother a transparent understanding of how they saw the same *data* and made the *same assumptions* but *inferred* different probabilities about the trip home.

The trip home story was transparent in large part because the assumptions and data were clearly stated, but this rarely is the case in the real world outside of made-up stories. In fact, assumptions are rarely stated, and unstated assumptions are at the root of many of the most heated arguments that regularly derail decision-making meetings. And the higher the stakes and level of uncertainty—recall the spectrum--the more emotions and biases push data to the side.

Consider, for example, stakeholders from different parts of an organization arriving at a meeting that begins with a common information base. But beyond the shared data, each participant understands it from the perspective of their own biases and interests. So, they assess it differently and make their own conclusions about what can be inferred from it and at what level of probability. More often than not, the fact that players have not stated their assumptions to their colleagues, or even understand they have any assumptions to state, only fuels the differences and undermines communication, leaving the group stuck in place and settling for a weakly supported consensus or making no decision.

Let's look at an another more realistic example of how the absence of unstated assumptions can play out in the intelligent analytic process (A + B →C). Assume here that the assumptions are unstated. The focus is the potential for implementing badly needed economic reforms.

Here is the inference:

- "Reporting over the last three months indicates that the new finance minister is determined to implement important pro-market economic reforms and has the president's strong backing, so the government is highly likely to come to an agreement with the IMF."

- Multiple assumptions related to the finance minister's and the president's real intentions, or the willingness of union leaders to go along, underpin this inference ("highly likely") and, again, the validity of the assumptions hinges on the data that supports them.

- And so, the discussion begins to answer the question: To what extent is the minister prepared to cut a deal with the IMF (highly likely, likely, or unlikely)? Well, it all depends on how each stakeholder determines whether the data closely supports the assumptions and moves the inference closer toward being a fact.

As a result, arguments interpreting the data or how well it supports an unstated assumption can be prolonged and shift quickly from a focus on the data to a focus on personalities without resolution, sometimes for months or even years on the really big analytic challenges. Think of the lost time and mental energy, and the damaged relationships caused by this problem. Worse, think about the audience: did that executive decision maker get the best possible response to the KIQ or a consensus that did not really help anyone?

Agreed-Upon Caveats Create a Continuum of Estimated Probability

To bring additional rigor, transparency, and consistency to estimating probability, analysts in the US intelligence services have used a standard set of agreed-upon terms intended to signal to the audience the likelihood that an event or development will occur. (ODNI ICD, 2015, 2016) Before the adoption of this standard, the meaning of caveats such as probably, highly likely, and highly unlikely, varied widely among and within the US intelligence services and was the source of endless arguments. While the mandated terminology has not resolved these differences or prevented some heated discussions among analysts, it has provided them and the audience with a sense of scale. There are two approaches. Figure 20 maps caveats on a continuum. Figure 21 is a table that includes additional caveats analysts have used for decades to characterize the estimated probability of inferences.

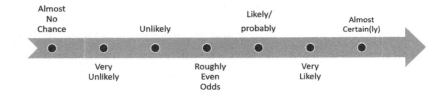

Figure 20. The continuum of ODNI's vocabulary of probability.

Almost No Chance	Very Unlikely	Unlikely	Roughly Even Odd	Likely	Very Likely	Almost Certainly
Remote	Highly Improbable	Improbable	Roughly Even Odds	Probable Probably	Highly Probable	Nearly Certain
01 – 5 %	05 – 20%	20 – 45%	45 – 55%	55 – 80%	80 – 95%	95 – 99%

Figure 21. Aligns caveats with likelihood expressed as percentages (source: Intelligence Community Directives [ICD] 203).

The decision to take this approach in the book is controversial among practitioners inside and outside the US intelligence services because, for some, it gives the audience an unwarranted sense of confidence. For other critics, the percentages just invite pressure for more precision, which can easily move analysts beyond fact-based reporting. Indeed, it is hard to resist when a senior executive asks an analyst to venture an opinion or more likely respond to a hypothetical "what if." Without an anchor in the reporting, however, an audience's selective listening can quickly in their minds turn the analyst's answer into a fact. That said, for all its potential pitfalls, the percentage scale beats the alternative—random unexplained and unexplainable caveated estimates and endless arguments—for two important reasons.

- First, intelligence analysis has repeatedly emphasized that the estimates of probability are dynamic, changing with reporting, and the scale at least gives readers a sense of the possibility of other outcomes.

■ Second, transparency matters, and the book will show in subsequent chapters that the disciplined process of estimating probability is a deliberate and conscious one. Figure 22 sets out the multiple terms that are used to caveat inferences—to express how close an assumption is to being a fact (ICD, 203; 2015).

ODNI's Caveats Tied to Specific Percentages	Caveats That Express Conditional Probability
• Remote • Very Unlikely • Unlikely/Even Chance • Probably/Likely • Very Likely • Almost Certainly	• Might • Would • Could • Maybe/May • Can
In Descending Order: Other Caveats Analysts Use to Convey Decreasing Degrees of Probability • Underscores • Indicates • Points to • Suggests	**Meaningless Caveats** • A chance • Cannot dismiss • It's conceivable • Perhaps • In my view/opinion • We believe/In our judgment (which express collective assessments of probability)

Figure 22. These caveats replace the arrow (→) symbol in the inference construct A + B → C.

Setting aside the ODNI's caveats in the upper left, here is an explanation of the other three quadrants, with examples. Caveats in the upper right quadrant (conditional probability) are known formally as modal verbs, or words of conditional probability, which express the possibility of an event occurring. Each has a specific meaning relative to expressing the probability of other less likely outcomes. In Intelligent Analysis, however, these caveats must be followed by "because," which signals an explanation of conditions that make it a plausible outcome. Absent such explanations, readers are left to sort out why or how the inference is a realistic assessment.

■ ***Example (correct use of conditional):*** The new subway routes could quickly force cab drivers off the roads because of reduced long-haul fares into the city that make up over half their revenue.

■ *Example (incorrect use of conditional):* The new subway routes may/could/might/should quickly force cab drivers off the roads. (No reason is given.)

Terms listed in the lower right quadrant (murky and unhelpful) are banned from Intelligent Analysis. They are weak and misleading substitutes for a clear judgment and are often used to obscure a lack of evidence and to convince readers that expertise or an opinion alone is enough of a reason to support an assessment, which of course is not true. In fact, they are just guessing or predicting.

Example: Despite multiple reports and other anecdotal information, we cannot dismiss (or there is a chance, we believe, in our judgment, in our view, in my opinion there may be) another outcome in the election.

Caveats in the lower left quadrant are part of the vocabulary as well. They appear arbitrary but they are understood among the US intelligence services and used extensively as another way of signaling the estimate of probability. The terms are listed in relative order of certainty, ranging from the more tentative term suggests to underscores or indicates, which express more certainty..

Example: Over the last six months, park attendance has increased significantly, and multiple reliable sources report a 20 percent increase in climbing-related accidents during the same period, which suggests/indicates/underscores that inexperience is behind the spike in climbing-related accidents in the park.

Which caveat is used depends on the strength of the quantitative and qualitative data, including perhaps medical records and interviews with injured individuals and witnesses.

Assumptions Are a Mine Field: Rules to Avoid Traps

Assumptions are at the heart of estimating probability. Their central role, however, also means they pose the greatest risk to the accuracy of the message given to decision makers in the B.L.U.F.'s lead inference. These rules, some of which already have been introduced, point out the most serious potential pitfalls.

Rule 1: Be sure assumptions are clearly stated.

Clearly articulating assumptions in writing forces you to think through the reasoning behind your estimated probability. It also makes your reasoning transparent to your audience and keeps the focus on the data, not personalities. And it has become common among the US intelligence services to state assumptions in even short assessments if there are wide differences among stakeholders. In addition, experienced senior audiences sometimes ask for assumptions so they can better understand the arguments.

Rule 2: Assumptions should be stated positively.

As the book has already made clear, assumptions are conditions that must exist, not conditions that must not exist, which could number in the dozens. The example below illustrates what happens when they are stated in the negative.

The inference: Supply lines are secure, and labor relations and global demand are steady, so the company will likely meet this year's 10 percent growth target.

The forecast is based on the following five (negative) assumptions:

- Supplies of critical materials are *not* interrupted.

- Material prices *don't* increase more than 2 percent.

- There are *no* strikes.

- Demand *does not* fall.

- There is *no* trade war between the US and China.

This list could on indefinitely to include list all the assumptions that must not persist to sustain the inference's (likely) forecast, but this formulation does not help identify the assumptions that *must* persist. The difference is not simply semantic. The good news is that these negatives can be easily recast in positively stated assumptions, which also facilitates the process of testing them. For example, the first assumption might read, "Supplies of critical materials remain readily available."

Rule 3: Limit key assumptions to no more than five or six.

This point was raised earlier in the chapter, but it's worth repeating. Starting out with an extensive list of working assumptions is important because it allows analysts to think broadly about what will determine the outcome (what's next). After the brainstorming, the list has to be narrowed to no more than five or six based on structured discussions among stakeholders about which assumptions are the most important to support the inference at the estimated level of probability. This winnowing down process is critical because the more conditions that must persist to support the inference's level of probability, the less control there is over the outcome. To be clear, it's not that the added assumptions are unimportant, but it does mean that the analysts have decided they are not as essential in developing the assessment.

Let's go back to the last example and see what happens when the list goes beyond six.

The inference: Supply lines are secure, and labor relations and global demand are steady, so the company will likely meet this year's 10 percent growth target.

The forecast is based on the following five (now positive) assumptions:

- Supplies of critical materials remain stable.

- Material prices are limited to 2 percent.

- Labor peace prevails.

- Demand remains steady.

- Trade relations between the US and China are improving.

Now add:

- Shipping lanes remain open.

- Trucks are available as needed.

- Banks continue to support the US with financing.

- Company leadership remains intact.

- Ports are well maintained.

The key assumptions—the most important conditions that must hold—now double to 10. The company cannot reliably assume that all 10 conditions will hold. As a result, the estimated probability that the company will hit its growth target (likely will) no longer accurately reflects the implied estimated probability in the inference. Even odds or unlikely might be more consistent with the reporting on all 10 assumptions.

Rule 4: New information must be continually integrated into the analysis.

Assumptions can become "frozen" when analysts fail to modify their expressed level of probability in the face of new information. Estimating probability that an event or development will occur must be a fluid process. If an analyst resists change—and this happens—they could consciously or unconsciously start to look for, or give credence to, only data that reinforces their position.

In fact, failure to change the estimated probability in the face of new data is as dangerous as formulating a KIQ that answers the question in the question. In disregarding new information, you run the risk of misleading the audience who may well make decisions assuming the analysis is accurate and consistent with the current reporting. Consider the potential consequences of your stubbornness and, if you are still clinging to your assessment in the face of new data, consider another line of work.

A corollary to Rule 4: As new information arrives and is integrated into the text, make sure to avoid "probability drift," explained in Chapter 1. To repeat, this problem occurs when reported data signals a change in the estimated probability of an event. For example, if new reporting signals a change from *likely* to *highly likely*, then adjustments must be made throughout the text. Unless this is done, the assessment will force the audience to play analyst to determine the analyst's intent. There are no easy fixes.

EXERCISE:
Identify the Assumptions that Underpin Your Own Inference

Let's turn to your project in an exercise where you identify the assumptions that underpin your B.L.U.F.'s lead inference.

Before starting here is an example you can follow as a model for your own work. We return to the NADA model B.L.U.F. Here is the inference repeated:

> The NADA PR head says tax cuts prevented a steeper decline in auto sales in 2018, but with the bump gone vehicle sales in 2019 will slip below 17 million vehicles for the first time in four years, which very likely means dealers and manufacturers will continue to recalibrate production targets and incentives as continuing shifts toward SUVs and trucks and rising prices and interest rates prompt renewed focus on used cars.

Notional Working Assumptions:

- Manufacturers continue incentives at an acceptable level.

- Price differential between new and used vehicles remains steady.

- Tax breaks remain unchanged.

- New car inventories are sufficient to meet customer demands.

- Gas prices remain low.

- NADA's sales predictions are correct.

- Tariffs on auto imports stabilize domestic supplies.

- Interest rates continue to rise.

- Sedans continue to slip in popularity.

Notional Key Assumptions:

1. Tax breaks remain unchanged

2. Gas prices remain low.

3. Interest rates continue to rise.

4. Sedans continue to slip in popularity.

5. Price differential between new and used vehicles remains steady.

Notional Linchpin Assumption:

- Sedans continue to slip in popularity.

Now, it's your turn. Here's one more reminder to help get you started:

- Assumptions are conditions that must persist to support your most likely outcome expressed in the inference at the level of certainty (language from the vocabulary of probability) based on the best available information at the time of writing. To help you stay on track keep asking yourself:

What conditions must persist in order to sustain my lead inference at the expressed (with a caveat) estimated level of probability.

INSTRUCTIONS:
Do the exercise in the sheets below or on your computer.

For now this is a two-step process. The third step follows your work on the Key Assumptions Check in the chapter 9.

Refer back to your own inference and make any changes. Then make a copy and enter it on your worksheet here:

_____
_____
_____

Step 1: Identify at least 8 or 10 working assumptions. Make sure they are stated positively and easily understood.

Step 2: From the working assumptions, choose the five or six that you think best support the level of probability expressed in your inference. These should be the assumptions you think best support the level of probability and the most important conditions that must persist in order to support the level of probability that the development or event expressed in your inference will occur.

Step 3: In the next chapter, we will use another framework to determine the linchpin assumption(s).

Step 1: List working assumptions. Try for at least 8 or 10. See the model after the exercise for ideas.

1. _____

2. _____

3. _____

4. _____

5. _____

6. _____

7._____

8._____

9._____

10._____

Step 2: Determine key assumptions. From the list of working assumptions, determine the five or six assumptions most important to supporting the estimated probability. Think this through!

1._____

2._____

3._____

4._____

5._____

6._____

Step 3: After completing work in chapter 9 determine linchpin assumptions. Think about which assumption(s) might be the linchpin assumption(s).

_____

_____

Gauging Data's Reliability: Critical Second Phase in Estimating Probability

The US intelligence services use a measure called the *level of confidence* (LOC) to express their assessment of the quality of the data supporting an assumption. This important gauge is expressed separately from the level of certainty and impacts probability differently. Think of the LOC as an expression of *"how do we know what we know."* Statements of the LOC are mandated in the 2004 Intelligence Reform and Prevention of Terrorism Act. The mandated LOC measure is in place because leaders in the US intelligence services saw that analysts, consciously or not, sometimes lowered their estimates of probability because of hesitation about the quality of the information underpinning their assumptions at the time of drafting. The audience, of course, would be unaware of the hesitancy, raising the risk of seeing an incomplete assessment (ICD 203).

- Expressing the LOC is not always required but is used most often when the reliability of the data helps to put the estimate of probability in context, especially when dealing with tough analytic questions.

- To avoid confusion, the probability estimate and the LOC must be expressed in separate sequential sentences. The first sentence expresses the estimated probability that an event or development will take place based on available information at the time of drafting. The next sentence must be a separate statement expressing the reliability of the information that underpinned the assumptions.

Specifically, the mandate stipulates that:

- "Judgments [assessments or inferences] are not intended to imply that we have proof that shows something to be a fact." In addition, the mere statement of an inference by itself does not mean it's accurate beyond the point in time the inference was drafted."

Consider, for example, this inference (exaggerated for effect):

> The car in the showroom looks great and the dealer has shown us a list of all the work that was done on the car and the Carfax report, so the vehicle is highly *likely* to be a good purchase.

The weight of the evidence—the dealer's word and the repair list, the Carfax report—all indicate that the data supports the inference. The next question, however, needs to be a consideration of the reporting's reliability. The Carfax report is certainly solid but can the same be said for either the dealer's reputation or the list of fixes? So, without the LOC statement the buyers have to accept the data which raises the risk that the car is not as advertised.

Three Levels of Confidence Explained with Examples

To help analysts gauge the reporting's LOC, the National Intelligence Council (NIC), which is part of the ODNI'S staff, has created a scale that can be used to describe the LOC and what it means for the validity of the inferences. Figure 23 illustrates the scale.

High Confidence	• The judgments are based on high-quality information, and/or the nature of the issue makes it possible to render a solid judgment. But • A "high confidence" judgment is not a fact and there is still risk of being wrong.
Moderate Confidence	• The information is credibly sourced and plausible, but not of sufficient quality or corroborated sufficiently to warrant a higher level of confidence.
Low Confidence	• The information's credibility and/or plausibility is questionable. • The information is too fragmented or poorly corroborated to make solid inferences. • We have significant concerns or problems with the sources.

Figure 23. The level of confidence in the information is provided in a separate sentence from the inference's estimated probability (ICD 203, National Intelligence Council, 203).

Figure 24 illustrates how the LOC looks in practice in a declassified Intelligence Community Assessment on global water security published in 2012 (ICA, "Water"). Note that in the first key judgment (A), the level of certainty is high, based on what is known, but there is only a moderate level of confidence in the sourcing because of gaps in the information. These two statements stand as separate characterizations.

Water Security: Key Judgments Separate Probability from Level of Confidence

A. We assess that during the next 10 years, water problems will contribute to instability in states important to US national security interests. Water shortages, poor water quality, and floods by themselves are unlikely to result in state failure. However, water problems—when combined with poverty, social tensions, environmental degradation, ineffectual leadership, and weak political institutions—contribute to social disruptions that can result in state failure.

*We have **moderate confidence** in our judgment as we have reliable open-source reporting on water pricing and infrastructure investments and reliable but incomplete all-source reporting on water quality.*

B. We assess that a water-related state-on-state conflict is unlikely during the next 10 years. Historically, water tensions have led to more water-sharing agreements than violent conflicts. However, we judge that as water shortages become more acute beyond the next 10 years, water in shared basins will increasingly be used as leverage; the use of water as a weapon or to further terrorist objectives also will become more likely beyond 10 years.

*We have **high confidence** in our judgments because there are excellent all-source reports on future water shortages and a well-established pattern of water problems aggravating regional tensions.*

Figure 24: Note the clear separation of the estimated probability from the LOC.

Here is an example from daily life that is highly likely to resonate with at least some of you. It involves a decision about buying a house in a new development.

- You arrive at the sales office with a set of assumptions (conditions that must persist). For example, the location is perfect, the areas already developed look good, the house's construction looks solid, and interior finishes appear to be high quality. The sales agent shows you brochures promising coming amenities, such as a pool/community center and nearby grocery store, to be built within a year.

- Reviewing your assumptions and the agent's pitch, you would be highly likely to buy the home. On reflection, however, you stop and consider the reliability of the information about the construction and promised facilities that clinched the deal. How much confidence can you have that the information is reliable? It came from a sales agent and your own inspection. We probably should wait and gather some additional information on the developer's performance elsewhere and the sales agent's relationship with the builder.

- Note the difference: The probability that the house is perfect is highly likely, but confidence in the information on the developer is much less so. You need to fill the gaps with additional data.

The two-sentence revised inference could look something like this:

- The quality of construction is good, and the promise of community amenities is a real plus, so we are highly likely to buy it. I have only *moderate confidence* in my estimated probability (*highly likely*) because while the information I have so far seems credible, it comes from the sales agent and I need corroboration and higher-quality information before closing the deal.

The Source Assessment Framework Focuses on the LOC

Intelligence assessments rely on multiple sources and the Source Assessment Framework will help analysts be more deliberate in assessing the sourcing for each key assumption. Here are some criteria to consider in assessing the LOC you can have in your data:

- Credentials: What Does the Author Know About the Subject?
- Objectivity : Does the Author Have an Agenda?
- Documentation: Where Did the Author Get the Information?
- Timeliness: When Was the Material Written?
- Review and Editing: Was the material peer reviewed for publication?
- What is the reputation of the media where the source first appeared?

Let's review the working assumptions we just developed for the NADA article. Recall that the analyst is tasked with making a recommendation to the managing director of whether to invest in auto stocks. To meet the requirement the analyst has decided to assess the sources to provide a level of confidence measure. Just looking at the completed source assessment illustrates the wide range of reliability to address the managing director's concerns.

1. B.L.U.F.'s Lead Inference	2. Name of Source	3. Assessment of Source Reliability	4. Source Rating 1–10 (Highest)
New vehicle sales in 2019 will slip below 17 million vehicles for the first time in four years, because a steeper decline in new auto sales in 2018 was only prevented by one-time tax cuts. As a result, car buyers will focus anew on used cars, due to continuing shifts toward SUVs and trucks and rising new car prices and interest rates			
—Below are the working assumptions that must persist to support the inference's estimated probability.			
• Manufacturers continue new vehicle incentives at an acceptable level. • Price differential between new and used vehicles remains steady. • New car inventories are sufficient to meet customer demands. • Tariffs on auto imports stabilize domestic supplies. • Sedans continue to slip in popularity. • NADA's sales predictions are correct.	NADA	Reliable. NADA has a good track record of data-driven auto industry analysis.	8
• Tax breaks remain unchanged. • Gas prices remain low. • Interest rates continue to rise.	NADA	Uncertain. NADA does not have any special insight into the direction of these economic variables.	3
			Overall Assessment

Figure 25. The Source Assessment Framework helps organize developing a level of confidence in your sources.

Here are explanations of the columns:

Column 1: Write down your key assumptions.

Column 2: Enter each data source used in making that assumption.

Column 3: This can be a short comment.

Column 4: Rate the source. A subjective rating but think of this way:

Rating of 1–3 = low confidence

Rating of 4–6 = moderate confidence

Rating of 7–10 = high confidence

EXERCISE:
Gauge the LOC in Your Own Lead Inference's Sources

INSTRUCTIONS:

Now use the Source Assessment Framework and column explanations in figure 26 above.

This is a two-step exercise.

Step 1: Assess your sources.

Use the blank source assessment below or on your computer.

1. B.L.U.F.'s Lead Inference	2. Name of Source(s)	3. Assessment of Source Reliability	4. Source Rating 1–10 (Highest)
Enter draft lead inference here.			
Then enter the key assumptions that must persist to support it.			
	Source Source Source		
1			
2			
3			

1. B.L.U.F.'s Lead Inference	2. Name of Source(s)	3. Assessment of Source Reliability	4. Source Rating 1–10 (Highest)
4			
5			
			Overall Assessment

Step 2: When it's filled in:

Fill in the blanks in the statement below.

- Give the LOC in the reporting an overall rating based on the National Intelligence Council's scale (high, moderate, or low).
- Go back to your inference.
- Recheck the inference to make sure the caveat that characterizes the estimated probability is correct for now. Write your draft inference again.

_____

_____

_____

_____

- Now add a second sentence directly following the summary inference expressing your level of confidence. For a model, see the example below. Just use the information you have collected to date. If you are not sure yet, assess the information you have collected so far. As a guide you can fill in the blank in this statement lifted from the NIE on water.

Model sentence:

We have ____(high, medium, low) confidence in our estimated level of probability of the B.L.U.F.'s lead inference because there are (cite sources) _____reports on _____.

CHAPTER NINE

Key Assumptions Check Tests Assumptions, Validates Estimate of Probability, Level of Confidence

> "Rechecking assumptions can be valuable at any time prior to finalizing judgments, to ensure that the assessment does not rest on flawed premises."
>
> —US Government, *A Tradecraft Primer: Structured Analytic Techniques for Improving Intelligence Analysis*

SUMMARY

Main Points

The Key Assumptions Check (KAC):

- Relies on structured evidence-based discussions to de-bias the analysis.

- Incorporates both the level of certainty and the reliability of quantitative and qualitative data, then measures each assumption's individual and then combined impact on the inference's estimated level of probability (likely, highly likely, or unlikely) that the event or development will occur; essentially, how close the assumption is to being a fact.

- Uses numerical ratings in the KAC to express the group's assessment. One important outcome is the selection of the linchpin assumption(s), the one or two assumptions deemed most critical to the inference's estimated probability.

- For example, weak and unreliable evidence supporting a linchpin assumption points to a critical vulnerability that requires mitigation.

KEY ASSUMPTIONS CHECK	[The inference being tested]				
1. Write out each assumption that underpins the inference: *What conditions must persist to maintain the validity of my most likely outcome at the estimated level of probability?*	2. How strongly does the evidence support the inference's estimated probability? (1-10 highest)	3. What is the level of confidence in the evidence? (1-10)	4. Would this assumption's failure cause any others to fail? (1-10)	5. What is the impact on inference's estimated probability if the assumption doesn't hold? (1-10)

Key Takeaways

- The KAC's structured discussions leverage expertise, foster collaboration across departments, and ensure that all voices are heard.

- Analysts complete their own KAC using a model scenario as a guide.

CHAPTER 9:
Key Assumptions Check Tests Assumptions,
Validates Estimate of Probability, Level of Confidence

"Rechecking assumptions can be valuable at any time prior to finalizing judgments, to ensure that the assessment does not rest on flawed premises. Identifying hidden assumptions can be one of the most difficult challenges an analyst faces, as they are ideas held—often unconsciously —to be true and, therefore, are seldom examined and almost never challenged."

—US Government, *A Tradecraft Primer: Structured Analytic Techniques for Improving Intelligence Analysis*

Goal: To be able to demonstrate the use of the KAC to identify key and linchpin assumptions based on a set of criteria that further refines the estimate of probability in your lead inference.

Objectives

At the end of this chapter, you will be better able to:

- Explain how the levels of certainty, and confidence in, the information impact the validity of the assumptions and the inference's estimate of probability.

- Evaluate the estimated level of probability of the inference that leads your B.L.U.F.

- Follow a scenario in this chapter and the next to see how a decision-making process integrates the KAC end to end.

Key Assumptions Check Integrates Levels of Certainty and Confidence

The level of certainty of the evidence and the level of confidence in the reliability of the evidence underpinning your assumptions are both crucial factors in determining the estimated level of probability that the event or development will occur. To bring more rigor to determining key and linchpin assumptions, the US intelligence services have for decades used the KAC framework. Specifically, the KAC structures data-driven discussions against a set of criteria to gauge in relative rank order how each key assumption can impact the inference's estimated probability. It allows analysts to measure the impact of both the reporting itself and the LOC in the reporting supporting the assumptions and the inference (Tradecraft Primer, 2009; Davis, 1997; Heuers, 1999).

Use of the KAC framework matters most when the audience's KIQ touches on a subject where there are significant differences among multiple stakeholders. Those differences can be fleshed out and tested using KAC criteria in structured discussions.

The KAC has two other important qualities:

- *First, the KAC de-biases the analysis.* It can help filter out emotions and biases and focus discussions on the data, not on personalities.

- *Second, the KAC is both a quantitative and qualitative tool.* That is, the numerical ratings used in the KAC to rate the inference's different dimensions are a result of structured, evidence-based discussions—in contrast to big or predictive data analytics--that leverage expertise and diverse views, foster collaboration across different components, and help ensure that all voices are heard.

For this reason, the US intelligence services label the KAC a "formal assumptions check" because the discussions are tightly structured and part of a managed process. The KAC can be used by a single analyst but remaining objective can be a challenge. It's best used with at least one collaborator, and the tool is even more effective when used in a team setting and that is how this book uses it.

The KAC Unpacks Assumptions

Figure 26 shows the blank KAC template. The scale for each column is 1–10, with 10 as the highest rating. As you work through the KAC, it's important to keep in mind that the KAC's purpose is to test the implied (→) relationship between the facts and the inference which is expressed in the estimated probability that the development or event will take place. That is to say, how close the evidence comes to making the inference a fact.

1. Write out each assumption that underpins the inference: *What conditions must persist to maintain the validity of my most likely outcome?*	2. How strongly does the evidence support the inference's estimated probability? Assign a rating (1-10)	3. What is the level of confidence in the evidence? (1-10)	4. Would this assumption's failure cause any others to fail? (1-10)	5. What is the impact on the inference's estimated probability if the assumption doesn't hold? (1-10)
One too many				

Figure 26. The KAC's 1–10 scale helps gauge the validity of the B.L.U.F.'s lead inference.

Each row is explained as follows, moving left to right.

Column 1: List key assumptions. Initially, all have the same weight. Linchpin assumptions will emerge later, from the completed framework. Remember to write the key assumptions in full sentences to make sure they are clearly stated and understood.

Column 2: Based on a review of the reporting supporting the level of probability Assign each assumption a strength of evidence rating. It answers the question: to what extent does the evidence available now support the assumption? When working as a group, reconciling diverse perceptions into a single rating in any of the columns can be time-consuming, but it is essential (no shortcuts).

Column 3: Assign a LOC rating to the source of the reporting. This rating answers the question : to what extent are the sources reliable? You are gauging known biases or the quality of the quantitative and qualitative reporting, including polls and surveys.

Column 4: This column measures the assumptions' interdependence, which is a reflection of the inference's complexity. That is whether one assumption's failure to hold up may cause a cascading effect across the other assumptions. It answers the question: to what extent would this assumption's failure create a cascading effect? Which is the most fragile?

Column 5: Rate the expected impact of each assumption on the inference's estimated probability. It answers the question: To what extent would the failure of this assumption to sustain its validity force a change in the caveat (more or less certainty) used to describe the relationship established in the inference.

- *Important note:* This rating is not a result of the averaging of the numbers in the previous columns, but a separate discussion that could require adjustments elsewhere. Trying to arrive at a column 5 rating by averaging the scores can be deceptive because the average might be higher for an assumption that would not impact the inference's estimated reliability.

Based on structured discussions after the KAC ratings are completed, a stand-back look at the assigned ratings reveals patterns that tell a story about the relationship between each assumption and the inference. Across each row, the KAC evaluates the reporting that supports each assumption, its impact on other assumptions, and then determines the impact on the inference. Moving down the columns, the data provides a comparative perspective on the assumptions' validity. Combined, they paint a powerful evidence-based test of the inference's estimate of probability. From this discussion flows the determination of the linchpin assumptions.

Application Scenario:
Global Real Estate Considers a Major Strategic Shift

Perspective

The following scenario demonstrates how this process unfolds. It begins in this chapter and continues in chapter 10.

Note: For instructional purposes, this scenario depicts a degree of consensus that does not generally reflect the internal dynamics that operate within the framework of structured analytic discussions, where differences of opinion are both encouraged and valued. In the "real world," sticking to this process can be challenging, which is why a facilitator can be important to ensuring a useful outcome. This dynamic and how to manage it, and dissenting perspectives, are discussed in detail at the end of chapter 10.

The setting: Global is a large commercial real estate company based in the Northeast. It started to expand on the West Coast last year and now sees an opportunity to move into another new market in Charlotte, North Carolina, with the purchase of a large office building in a developing part of the city.

- The first part begins with the acquisition team's initial upbeat recommendation which the board wants to review. A facilitator comes in to lead the review, which begins with working assumptions and ends with the completed KAC.

- The second part starts in the next chapter. It shows how to use the KAC's results to develop the most likely outcome, implications for the company, mitigation strategies to manage -not avoid- risk, and indicators of success to help track the "health" of the assumptions that underpin the inference.

The audience: Global's Chief Risk Officer (CRO), who reports to the CEO that will make the ultimate decision on the purchase.

- *The agreed-upon intelligence question:* To what extent would the purchase of the Acme Building in Charlotte strengthen Global's position in that growing market?

- *The participants:* Drawn from multiple stakeholders across the company (i.e., marketers, economists, engineers, finance experts, and, of course, lawyers).

The CRO Questions the Team's Initial Assessment

The team convenes for half a day, holds some discussions, and decides to send this assessment to the CRO.

- The acquisition team has reviewed all relevant information and has determined that the Acme Building's location and terms of the sale indicate that the purchase is highly likely to position Global in a key market for long-term growth.

Here is how the inference breaks down:

Fact A: The Acme Building's location

+

Fact B: and the terms of sale

Implies (→) C: *that the purchase is highly likely to position Global in a key market for long-term growth.*

The CRO is cautious and wants to make sure the team fully considered the question given the high stakes. The CRO asks the team, to "stress test" its assessment for the CEO. The CRO, who has read our book, also specified that a facilitator trained in SATs should guide the team's discussions.

The Process Begins: Here's How It Unfolds

The facilitator starts with an explanation of SATs and how the team will proceed.

Representatives from all the key stakeholders are around the table. The facilitator meets with the group, recaps the team's work to date, explains the line of march and restarts the process. Here is how it unfolded.

Step 1: Based on preliminary research focused on the KIQ the team develops a list of working assumptions. Here is the list in no particular order:

- Charlotte will sustain its current level of economic growth at 4 percent annually.

- The developing area around the Acme Building will continue to attract an affluent population.

- The demand for office space will grow at 5 percent annually.

- Other properties will be available for acquisition within a 20-mile radius of Acme.

- Current tenants in the building will extend their leases even with a 10 percent increase in rent that starts after the building is upgraded.

- Occupancy rates will remain at least at 85 percent.

- The Acme Building will be competitive with other new and existing office space.

- Positive engineering assessments of the building's current systems and infrastructure are accurate.

- The building can accommodate planned renovations and IT upgrades, including residential and retail units.

- The lender's interest rate will remain at 3.75 percent.

- Global will be able to sustain its West Coast acquisition plans.

- Global is prepared to sustain significant losses from the acquisition.

- Global can staff maintenance and other support positions.

- The building's title is clear.

- Key Global personnel will be willing to relocate to build on the acquisition.

Step 2: The team selects key assumptions

The potential list is extensive. The team's discussion takes up most of a day during which it uncovered multiple unstated assumptions that made the list. Eventually it selects six key assumptions to list in column 1:

- Charlotte will sustain its current level of economic growth at 4 percent annually.

- Key Global personnel will be willing to relocate to build on the acquisition.

- Global will be able to sustain its West Coast acquisition plans.

- Positive engineering assessments of the building's current systems and infrastructure are accurate.

- The Acme Building will be competitive with other new and existing office space.

- Other properties will be available for acquisition within a 20-mile radius of Acme.

The facilitator explains that after the KAC exercise the team will have sufficient data to select the linchpin assumptions, those that matter most to the validity of the estimated probability.

The facilitator turns to the KAC template, ties it to the last exercise and explains the meaning of each column and the ground rules for determining the ratings. The key assumptions are already entered in column 1 of in full sentences. The process of filling in the ratings in next four columns begins. For our purposes, although the brief summaries of the steps below do not capture the flow and intensity of the discussions around each assumption and the ratings in each column, team members generally stick to their areas of expertise and trust each other's assessments. The team moves methodically under the facilitator's watchful eye. In sequence, the team moves to:

Step 3 – Column 2: *Reviews the level of certainty in the evidentiary base.*

All the participants walk the team through what they know from each of their areas of expertise.

Step 4 – Column 3: *Reviews their level of confidence in the reporting.*

During these discussions, the variations in the data's quality begin to surface.

Step 5 – Column 4: *Rates the impact each assumption has on the others.*

This next step is the first time that team members start to step out of their areas of expertise. The discussions reveal some important differences among stakeholders about the which assumptions would have the most impact on the estimated probability of the inference if they failed.

Step 6 – Column 5: *Lastly focuses on overall impact of each assumption on the inference's estimated probability.*

Setting these ratings is the toughest part of the process because of the number of players and the outcome's implications for the team's assessment for the CRO and the CEO. Figure 27 shows the team's completed KAC.

Write out each assumption that underpins the judgment: *What conditions must persist to maintain the validity of my most likely outcome?*	How strongly does the evidence support the inference's estimated probability? (1-10)	What is the level of confidence in the reliability of the evidence? (1-10)	Would this assumption's failure cause any others to fail? (1-10)	What is the impact on the inference's estimated probability if the assumption doesn't hold? (1-10)
1. Charlotte will sustain its current level of economic growth at 4 percent annually	8	5	9	10
2. Key Global personnel will be willing to relocate to build on the acquisition	9	8	6	5
3. Global will be able to sustain its West Coast acquisition plans	8	8	6	6
4. Positive engineering assessments of the building's current systems and infrastructure are accurate	7	5	10	10
5. Other properties will be available for acquisition within a 20-mile radius of the Acme Building	9	9	6	6
6. Acme will be competitive with other new and existing office space	8	5	8	8

Figure 27. The team's new KAC raises unrecognized red flags.

The Team Looks for Patterns in the Data

The length and depth of the discussions was sobering and often difficult, as members sorted through each assumption's potential impact on the inference's estimated probability and the linchpins. Together the ratings told a story and the team needed to draw it out of the numbers. To help start the process, the facilitator assigned the members to collectively answer the following three questions (responses in chapter 10):

- Where is the team's lead inference most vulnerable? Identify the linchpins? Explain using the data.

- What are other important vulnerabilities the team now needs to consider? Explain using the data.

- Where does the team think its assessment is on comparatively secure footing? Explain using the data.

The team was instructed to answer the questions in full sentences using the data.
To be continued in next chapter.

EXERCISE:
Complete the KAC for Your Project and Adjust the Inference

Instructions:

- Insert the key assumptions for your project which you listed in chapter 8.

- Fill in the template with ratings. This part can be done on your own but the power of the KAC rests in the discussions about the ratings.

- Before moving on, however, go back to the inference in your B.L.U.F. that you re-wrote at the end of Chapter 8 and, as necessary, reassess the estimate of probability that the event or development will occur.

1. Write out each assumption that underpins the inference: *What conditions must persist to maintain the validity of my most likely outcome?*	2. How strongly does the evidence support the inference's estimated probability? Assign a rating (1-10)	3. What is the level of confidence in the evidence? (1-10)	4. Would this assumption's failure cause any others to fail? (1-10)	5. What is the impact on the inference's estimated probability if the assumption doesn't hold? (1-10)
One too many				

A reminder. As you complete the KAC keep in mind that, like the probability estimates discussed in chapter 8, the 1- 10 rating scale results are not intended to imply precision but rather to anchor, or frame, data-driven discussions which then become part of the team's work documentation. That said, a sense of scale helps analysts relate the numbers in each column to their impact on the validity of the inference.

■   If you're assigning KAC ratings on your own or working with a team of colleagues who are unfamiliar with the process of selecting KAC ratings, you can use the rating table provided in Appendix D as an anchor.

The story—and work on your project—picks up in the next chapter.

CHAPTER TEN

Key Assumptions Check Results Estimate Most Likely Outcome, Implications, Mitigation Strategies

> "There are those people who produce forecasts uncritically. When asked why they forecast, they answer, 'Well, that's what we're paid to do here.' My suggestion: get another job."
>
> —Nassim Taleb, *Black Swan*

SUMMARY

Main Points

- As explained in the last chapter, the KAC tests each assumption's soundness—how close it is to being a fact based on the evidence and its reliability. Structured discussions now draw on the KAC's results to develop the look ahead, which includes the B.L.U.F.'s last three elements that focus on the unknown.

- The patterns that emerge from the structured discussions shape a more complete, evidence-based assessment of the decision's soundness, including:

  - *The most likely outcome*, as well as a range of other possibilities: the "so what."

  - *An explanation of vulnerabilities*—including the most critical linchpin assumption(s)—and relative strengths where the decision is on safer ground.

  - *Implications for the organization* flow from the most likely outcome: why it matters, or the "so what of the so what."

  - *Mitigation strategies* to manage risk and uncertainty or exploit opportunities.

  - *Indicators of change,* another SAT that tracks the strategies' success (or lack thereof).

- A framework and a model scenario help analysts develop these elements for their projects. A final section discusses the importance of welcoming dissents from the assessment as expressed in the B.L.U.F.

Key Takeaways

Looking ahead carries risks: trust the process but anticipate obstacles like these:

- Criticsm of SATs and the intelligent analytic process.

- Pulling rank and shutting down discussion.

- Drawing inferences from inferences.

- Incorrect use of conditional caveats: might, could, should and may.

- Expressing over-confidence, unwarranted caution, and/or the need to compromise

CHAPTER 10:
Key Assumptions Check Results Estimate Most Likely Outcome,
Implications, Mitigation Strategies

"There are those people who produce forecasts uncritically. When asked why they forecast, they answer, 'Well, that's what we're paid to do here.' My suggestion: get another job."

—Nassim Taleb, *Black Swan*

Goal: To understand how the results of the KAC exercise become the basis for a forward-looking stress test of the inference's estimated probability before implementation, including analysis that identifies the most likely, and other possible, outcomes, points out where the decision is most and least vulnerable, develops mitigation strategies, and values dissenting views as part of the intelligent analytic process.

Objectives

At the end of this chapter, you will be able to:

- Explain how testing assumptions in the KAC exercise identifies the most likely and other possible outcomes.

- Use the KAC results to identify the most and least important risks to implementation.

- Suggest mitigation strategies to reduce risk and indicators to track their effectiveness.

- Create an environment where evidence-based dissent is valued and accepted as part of the analytic process.

KAC Results Shift Story from What's Known to What's Next

In Intelligent Analysis, the KAC's results and your revised inference drive development of the B.L.U.F's last three elements. These elements include the most likely outcome, implications for the organization, and mitigation strategies to blunt the impact of vulnerabilities and exploit any opportunities that might surface. Indicators of effectiveness are developed as needed.

This chapter shows how the flow unfolds when we return to the Global team's continuing effort to support the senior executive's decision-making. Be sure to note how the team members' analysis of the KAC results changes their assessment of the estimated level of probability that the Acme purchase will benefit Global. From that analysis, the team turns to drafting a transparent and defensible B.L.U.F. which includes what's known and what's next, including:

- Most likely outcome

- Implications for Global's long-term future

- Suggested mitigation strategies to influence the outcome

- Indicators to track the effectiveness (or ineffectiveness) of the mitigation strategies (drawn from: *Tradecraft Primer*, 2009; Davis, 1997; Heuer, 1999)

New Insights Emerge from KAC Data

Global Real Estate's assessment team is still tightly focused on reviewing its initial upbeat assessment of the Acme Building purchase. The next step is to draw on the KAC ratings to answer the facilitator's three questions and begin the process of assessing what to tell the audience about the look ahead—the "so what"—and then the implications for the board's decision—the "so what of the so what." Global's assessment team has completed their revised KAC and seen patterns that will require significant revisions to the initial optimistic assessment that buying the building is likely to position Global in a key market for long-term growth. Before turning to the exercise, the facilitator remarks on how effectively the team has used the KAC to minimize the biases and emotions that contributed to their initial discussion. Team members agree and point out the benefits they have seen in structured discussions.

The KAC exercise so far:

- Gave the team a set process that moved methodically through assessments of the evidence and quality of reporting.

- Encouraged a collaborative environment that ensured broad participation in the discussions.

- Kept the team focused on the answering the question.

- Made everyone's assumptions transparent and open to scrutiny.

- Managed group dynamics, including keeping the discussions evidence based and surfacing biases.

- Raised the visibility of the most critical—linchpin—assumptions.

- Pointed out where the assessment was most/least vulnerable.

- Set the stage for developing the outlook.

To help you move forward Figure 28 repeats the team's completed KAC.

Write out each assumption that underpins the judgment: *What conditions must persist to maintain the validity of my most likely outcome?*	How strongly does the evidence support the inference's estimated probability? (1-10)	What is the level of confidence in the reliability of the evidence? (1-10)	Would this assumption's failure cause any others to fail? (1-10)	What is the impact on the inference's estimated probability if the assumption doesn't hold? (1-10)
1. Charlotte will sustain its current level of economic growth at 4 percent annually	8	5	9	10
2. Key Global personnel will be willing to relocate to build on the acquisition	9	8	6	5
3. Global will be able to sustain its West Coast acquisition plans	8	8	6	6
4. Positive engineering assessments of the building's current systems and infrastructure are accurate	7	5	10	10

Table continued on next page

Write out each assumption that underpins the judgment: *What conditions must persist to maintain the validity of my most likely outcome?*	How strongly does the evidence support the inference's estimated probability? (1-10)	What is the level of confidence in the reliability of the evidence? (1-10)	Would this assumption's failure cause any others to fail? (1-10)	What is the impact on the inference's estimated probability if the assumption doesn't hold? (1-10)
5. Other properties will be available for acquisition within a 20-mile radius of the Acme Building	9	9	6	6
6. Acme will be competitive with other new and existing office space	8	5	8	8

Figure 28. Patterns in the team's KAC reveal important insights.

See chapter 9 to review.

KAC Results Provide Critical Insights into the Initiative's Complexity

Based on the KAC results, here are the team's responses to the three questions posed by the facilitator at the end of chapter 9.

Team's response to question 1
Where is the team's lead inference most vulnerable; which are the linchpin assumptions? Explain using the data.

The team decides that assumptions 1 (economic growth projections) and 4 (accuracy of engineering assessments) are the linchpin assumptions that expose the most critical vulnerabilities. The team reasoned that the growth estimates come from the city government and chamber of commerce and may well be optimistic. In addition, while Global's engineers have done their due diligence and found problems that need addressing, they also assert that it is an aging building and there could easily be costly problems that surface during the renovation.

Team's response to question 2
Beyond the linchpin assumptions, what other vulnerabilities does the board also need to consider? Explain using the data.

The team decides that assumption 6 (price competitiveness with other properties) is also an important vulnerability that needs to be managed. Based on Global's experience elsewhere, the team reasoned that if the renovation exceeds worst-case estimates, then setting leasing rates sufficient to recoup the costs or absorbing the costs to stay competitive could well wreak havoc with the company's long-term revenue projections. Also, the Acme Building deal could attract competing real estate management companies to the area.

Team's response to question 3

Where does the team think the acquisition team is on comparatively secure footing? Explain using the data.

The team decides that assumptions 2 (Global personnel willing to move to Charlotte), 3 (sustaining West Coast acquisitions), and 5 (other properties in area available for acquisition) could be more readily managed. They reasoned that internal survey results show that over half the current staff would transfer to take advantage of the city's schools and housing, and the strong local talent pool could fill any gaps. An assessment of real estate available outside of Charlotte shows multiple attractive properties in growing areas. And financing for the West Coast purchases is already in place.

With the three basic questions answered, the facilitator tells the team that the CRO and CEO want additional details on their reasoning behind each assumption supporting their shift and why it matters to the company's decision.

Team Explains Their Most Likely Outcome ("What's Next")

Note how the outlook—the "so what"—is starting to take shape. The analysis is so far firmly anchored in data with a combination of the KAC results and members' own expertise and experience. The use of the KAC also has made the reasoning behind the assessment transparent, defensible, and traceable. Each line and column tells a story.

Taking the next step the team assesses that the overall operating environment the acquisition team would have to navigate before closing the deal is more complex and less predictable than asserted in their benign initial judgment. The team restates its assessment and includes the LOC in the sourcing behind the assessment:

- "Drawing on a range of reliable data and diverse expertise, the team has determined that the purchase is likely to benefit Global, but important vulnerabilities need to be mitigated related to the city's positive economic forecast and the building's condition; other areas of concern are more manageable."

■ "We have high confidence that the initiative's most important vulnerabilities can be reexamined because other more independent economic reporting is available to check the city's forecast and specialized engineering companies can look more deeply at the building's internal systems and structural integrity."

We will learn later in the chapter that not everyone was on board with the team's responses. Again, dissents should be expected and welcomed, not buried.

Here is the team's more detailed explanations of how they grouped the assumptions. Note how the team uses the columns across the KAC to construct their responses.

Question 1: Where is the team's lead inference most vulnerable; which are the linchpin assumptions? Answer: Assumptions 1 and 4 are the linchpin assumptions.

■ *Assumption 1: Charlotte will sustain its current level of economic growth at 4 percent annually.* Explanation:

"City officials presented data that forecasted sustained annual economic growth rate of 4 percent, but the team's deeper look at the data raises questions about its accuracy. The team recognizes that slower-than-projected growth would undermine Global's revenue projections, which are the basis for moving into Charlotte with the Acme purchase."

■ *Assumption 4: Positive engineering assessments of the building's current systems and infrastructure are accurate.* Explanation:

"The engineering assessments overall indicate that the Acme Building, while dated, is sound and can accommodate Global's plans to update and market the building's office and retail space. In the past, Global has always benefited from a second set of engineering assessments that look more deeply into the infrastructure and the building's ability to be upgraded. This step is critical because any major problems uncovered during construction would cause significant cost overruns, delaying occupancy and undermining revenue and other critical assumptions built into the decision to make the purchase."

Question 2: Beyond the linchpin assumptions, what other vulnerabilities does the board also need to consider?

- **Assumption 6:** *The Acme Building is price competitive.* Explanation:

  "Current data on similar buildings indicates that Acme will be able to retain current tenants even with expected rent increases and attract new occupants, but slowdowns in economic growth or unexpectedly higher construction costs would impact other assumptions related to Global's revenue projections in Charlotte and the company's other plans for growth in the region."

Question 3: Where does the team think the board is on comparatively secure footing?

Answer: Assumptions 2, 3, and 5. Explanation: The board should watch for changes but at this point they don't need to address them.

- **Assumption 2:** *Local labor market will compensate for key Global personnel unwilling to relocate to Charlotte.* Explanation:

  "A survey of Global staff indicated initially high interest in relocating to Charlotte because of the area, housing, schools, and less hectic lifestyle, but personal lives can work against a move at decision time. Highly qualified personnel, however, are readily available locally and would bring their own unique expertise to Global, so even significantly lower employee interest would have little or no impact on the other assumptions and acquisition decision."

- **Assumption 3:** *Global will be able to sustain its West Coast acquisition plans.*

"The team is confident that Global has the financial resources and strong, well-documented banking relationships to support its ongoing West Coast acquisitions regardless of what happens in Charlotte, but even if the Acme Building deal collapses, Global would still be able to establish a footprint in the Charlotte area."

■ **Assumption 5:** *Other properties will be available for acquisition within a 20-mile radius of the Acme Building.* Explanation:

"The team's survey of official records of commercial property sales in and around Charlotte over the last three years points to considerable churn in the market, and while there are often multiple bidders, the large number of available buildings that meet Global's criteria means this assumption has no real dependencies and should have no impact on the board's decision."

Before moving on two team members tell the team that while they agree with how the assumptions have been rated at some point they want to revisit the selection of the linchpin assumptions. They see the engineering assessments as underestimating the risk to the company's success. They see them as the single most important—and only—linchpin. Old buildings hold surprises, and the engineering assessments need to dig more deeply into potential areas of concern much deeper, especially the ventilations and ability to accommodate significantly larger computer systems for a larger workforce. Potential cost overruns can run into the millions of dollars, threatening all the revenue projections that make the purchase the best step for moving into a new market. The CRO and the CEO need to understand the real magnitude of the risks. The team agrees to revisit the assessment as part of looking at the mitigation strategies.

CRO Now Wants Mitigation Strategies to Manage Risk, Track Progress

Intelligent Analysis is about identifying and managing risk and navigating uncertainty, not avoiding it. Only the audience—in this case the CRO and CEO--can determine their organization's risk tolerance. The team's outlook provided a balanced, evidence-based assessment that pointed out the benefits but also indicated that unchecked vulnerabilities could quickly outweigh any gains, and they are anxious to hear about any dissenting voices. To start, the board welcomed the team's assessment and opted to slow down the process. But developing a presence in Charlotte has been one of the company's highest priorities for long-term growth and stepping away is not an option. With that, the CRO asked the team to create a path that minimized the team's assessment of the two most critical risks. Again, the members' deep and broad expertise across the company and the real estate industry position them to recommend measures to meet the board's requirement. It is a two-step process.

- First, develop mitigation strategies. The goal is to develop an evidenced-based plan that reduces—not eliminates—the impact of the identified vulnerabilities. Then the board can decide their risk tolerance.

- Second, build a set of success measures, or indicators. Indicators track the strategies' effectiveness. To be most useful indicators require specific metrics and changes in the status of the assumptions. Reporting must be observable and readily accessible to stakeholders, who can track the indicators on their own. Indicators serve three functions. They:

  - Give the CEO and the team visibility into the success (or failure) of the mitigation strategies' impact on the two key vulnerabilities.

  - Track the "health" of the other assumptions to make sure there are no significant changes that would alter their status; what looks like a safe bet now can change quickly or more slowly over the longer term.

  - Help teams manage analytic differences over the most likely outcome, such as the questions raised about the building's condition. Rather than argue about priorities, the team decided to develop indicators to make sure it would spot any emerging trouble spots. The higher the uncertainty, the more this approach can help analysts manage differences and provide their audience with a complete assessment and path for moving forward.

The Mitigation and Indicator Framework in Figure 29 helps analysts be more deliberate and thorough in sorting out their thinking on risk. The framework s process needs to be used to track the other assumptions as well to monitor their validity.

Linchpin Assumptions (Plus 1, if needed)	1. Why Vulnerable	2. Mitigation Strategy	3. Specific Indicators We Would See If the Mitigation Strategy Is Working	4. Specific Indicators We Would See If the Mitigation Strategy Is Not Working	5. Comments
Linchpin assumption					
Linchpin assumption					
A third optional assumption					

Figure 29. The Mitigation and Indicator Framework.

What the columns mean:

Column 1: *The vulnerability.* What makes this a linchpin? Reading across the row, write out one or two sentences that describe why it's vulnerable.

Column 2: *The mitigation strategy.* Describe in detail what action needs to be taken.

Column 3: *Indicators the strategy is working.* Think of it this way: what would we expect to see if the strategy results in a positive change in any of the KAC ratings? The indicators are expressed as metrics based on observable data.

Column 4: *Indicators that the strategy is not working.* Again, expressed in metrics. These metrics are not just the opposite of those expressed in column 3.

Column 5: *Comments.* Included here are observations about the strategy or the metrics.

The detailed example in figure 30 shows what a completed framework would look like, but it uses an assumption that for now is considered safe. The choice is intended to reinforce the point that what looks manageable early on can shift to a higher concern. Note that the indicators are tied to specific metrics to make them transparent, observable, and traceable. Also, in developing mitigation strategies, the team avoids falling back on using a conditional vocabulary to caveat their suggestions. Remember that conditional vocabulary—*could, might, may, should*—adds no value without the required follow-on "because" that would explain with evidence why the step would mitigate the risk. Right, the table is long and detailed but that's the point: what's safe now can become critical and metrics are key to determining when steps need to be taken to mitigate the risk.

Assumption 2: Local labor market will compensate for key Global personnel unwilling to relocate to Charlotte.

Based on KAC results, the team reasoned that additional incentives would encourage moves and locals could fill any remaining gaps. These labor market indicators may seem obvious, but a shift in a negative direction could leave key positions unfilled.

Assumption 2	Vulnerabilities	Mitigation Strategies	Specific Indicators We Would See If the Mitigation Strategy Is Working	Specific Indicators We Would See If the Mitigation Strategy Is Not Working	Comments
Local labor market will compensate for key Global personnel unwilling to relocate to Charlotte.	Ninety days before the move, at least 25 mid- and VP-level positions are not filled. List of potential transfers falls below requirements. Local recruiting firms fail to present at least three qualified applicants for each position.	In Charlotte, hire multiple recruiting firms.	Recruitment firms provide sufficient résumés that meet hiring requirements for top three positions within 90 days to acquisition.	Recruitment firms provide less than six highly qualified applicants 60 days ahead of acquisition.	May broaden search area beyond Charlotte or plan for staff to work remotely.

Table continued on next page

Assumption 2	Vulnerabilities	Mitigation Strategies	Specific Indicators We Would See If the Mitigation Strategy Is Working	Specific Indicators We Would See If the Mitigation Strategy Is Not Working	Comments
		In Charlotte undertake major PR campaign to tout company.	Local press bolsters Global's visibility and attracts at least 50 to Global job fair and 15 candidates approach executive recruiters.	Recruitment falls below expectations (30 at job fair, 5 to recruiters). Expected influx of new companies shrinks talent pool.	May need to send out recruiters to specialized groups.
		Inside Global, intensify recruiting efforts and incentives to encourage relocation.	Initiative, including company-sponsored visits to the area for tours of schools and housing, convince seven key senior officers and rising stars to make the move.	Reports of poor local school ratings heighten existing reluctance to uproot families	Global may need to re-think how it's incentivizing senior and support staff to relocate.
		For local working-level positions, recruit at local colleges and universities and hold job fair.	Global's starting salaries and online praise for the positive work environment attract multiple candidates and recruiters to attend events and job fairs.	Competition for qualified candidates is more intense than expected and starting salaries fall behind competitors'.	Global can go beyond Charlotte area and recruit in areas where competition is less and local job markets are weak.

Figure 30. Mitigation strategies to manage staffing in Charlotte.

Well-developed sets of indicators can play two important roles across any organization.

- *A warning function* to spot *immediate threats.* These can include, for example, business and competitive intelligence, new product announcements, insider threats, mergers and acquisitions, and cyberattacks. For organizations with overseas interests, warnings would include labor and political unrest.

- *Assess longer-term trends.* These can include shifts in an organization's operating environment such as technology breakthroughs, developments in labor markets, demographic shifts, and legislation and compliance issues.

Warning: An Admonition: make sure that reports of immediate threats are anchored in reporting. As pointed out elsewhere in this book, the threshold for alerting the audience is low—as few as one or two reports is sufficient—but be careful in drafting. Warnings describe what, when, and how bad and no speculation.

Team's Revised Lead Paragraph Tells a Different Story

Thinking ahead to the report which team members owe the CEO, the facilitator returns to their original B.L.U.F. inference and asks them to draft a new lead paragraph. Here again, as a reminder, is the team's initial assessment:

> "The acquisition team has reviewed all relevant information and has determined that the building's location and terms of the sale indicate that the Acme purchase is highly likely to position Global in a key market for long-term growth."

Figure 31 returns the team to the B.L.U.F. template to recast its assessment. Note how the language mirrors the revised KAC's message. The team decides to retain both linchpin assumptions but give the two team members space to set out their position (discussed below). The indicators can easily track both developments.

Title	Charlotte's Growth Forecasts, Building's Condition Are Biggest Risks to Purchase
Inference summarizes the B.L.U.F..	Based on a range of reporting and Global's expertise the acquisition team assesses that purchasing the Acme Building is highly likely to benefit Global, provided that important vulnerabilities related to the city's economic forecast and the building's condition are mitigated; other areas of concern are more manageable. We have high confidence in our assessment because independent economic consultants raised questions about the forecast and the initial engineering report pointed to the potential for unseen problems.
What's the new development?	At the request of the CEO and CRO the acquisition team revisited its initial assessment of the Acme Building's viability as a first purchase in the Charlotte area.
Why now?	Specifically, the CRO wanted to the team to stress test its optimistic assessment using structured analytic techniques.
How does it work?	Using SATs and a skilled facilitator to manage the process the team restarted the process that reveals important new insights into the potential benefits and risks related to the purchase.
What's ahead ("so what")?	The team assesses that Global's best course for now is to slow down the acquisition process until the team can probe more deeply into these vulnerabilities.
What are the implications (the "so what of the so what")?	Slowing the process might well cost Global the opportunity to purchase the Acme Building, but Global has been in this situation before and still moved forward at great cost to the company.
What steps can be taken to mitigate risks and exploit and opportunities?	the team is in the process of developing mitigation strategies to deal with both the most important vulnerabilities, as well as lesser risks that can rise in importance later in the process.

Figure 31. Revised B.L.U.F. reflecting team's course correction.

Note how each sentence could be easily expanded into a separate paragraph or section, depending on length. The last section would comprise tables that recommend mitigation strategies and indicators for each key assumption, as well as pointing to other similar buildings available in the market.

Looking Ahead Carries Risks: Anticipate Resistance but Trust the Process

The Global acquisition assessment exercise described above went smoothly—too smoothly to mirror what generally happens in diverse groups trying to solve tough problems, whether under pressure or not. It was set up to illustrate how the process should unfold, albeit in an ideal environment. There was an important outcome for the company because:

- The facilitator was trained, understood the process, and kept the team on task.

- Everyone on the team supported the approach and accepted the ground rules.

- Senior executives were serious about looking for a second opinion

- Dissent was managed—no organizational silence buried different perspectives.

Years of experience in being part of and facilitating structured discussions, however, remind me that the ideal is just that. More often than not, there is at least one participant that does not believe in SATs, likes the old ways of decision analysis, and sits back with arms folded. Others may be more vocal, touting their seniority and experience and just as often clinging to their assumptions regardless of the reporting. Similarly, senior managers are often reluctant to cede authority or appear to be in need of decision support and they will simply regard the exercise as just that – an exercise. Just because you provide a well-documented assessment doesn't mean it will be welcome or followed which is their decision. You have done your job and the team's work is transparent, defensible, and repeatable.

The facilitator helped the team handle other challenges to the process as well. They surfaced largely as the team developed the most likely outcome. They included:

- *Challenges to the process itself.* The use of SATs to develop the outlook is questioned. Resistance on this point most typically comes from senior or more experienced participants. Touting their seniority and experience they just know what's next. And just as often cling to their assumptions regardless of the reporting.

- *Pressure to go beyond the reporting.* Inferences drawn from inferences is endemic, especially when the information base is thin. It can come from anyone in the group, but again most often the culprits are senior analysts who tout expertise and long experience and are convinced of their brilliance. SATs are meant to structure discussions and shift them away from personalities to the data. Push back.

- *Misuse of conditional caveats.* Recall that "because" must follow conditional caveats such as might, could, may, should, and maybe in order to transform speculation into an informed explanation of other possible outcomes. Force the issue with team members who want to do otherwise.

- *The risk of probability drift.* Endless arguments and fatigue breeds compromise. The back-and-forth can lead to changes in the estimated probability at different points in the text. This happens, which is why the team needs to revisit the entire text to ensure that decision-makers see a consistent message. There are no such things as easy fixes in Intelligent Analysis.

The process also helped the team avoid two other serious risks: overconfidence and unwarranted caution. Both happen.

- *Overconfidence.* It's just plain arrogance. Someone in the room pushes for an unwarranted and unsupportable probability estimate often with a raised voice, claims of deep experience, "just a gut instinct," or all of the above. If you opt to fold, be forewarned. Analysts are trading the safe harbor of Intelligent Analysis for a minefield when analysis becomes prediction and creates a ready path over the next cliff.

- *Unwarranted caution.* It's at the other end of the analytic spectrum and just as potentially dangerous. In these cases, analysts pull punches to avoid being wrong. "Probably" is the most overused word in Intelligent Analysis. It's supposed to be used only to signal that there are other possible outcomes, which is part of the process, but it's too often used as a hedge. Trouble arises when the estimated probability is lowered despite a strong evidentiary base built on high-quality reporting. This behavior can leave decisionmakers wondering what they are missing. If there are alternative outcomes, explain them.

The lesson here is don't hedge your assessment and don't be afraid to be wrong. Yes, you can be wrong for the right reasons even if you followed every tenet of Intelligent Analysis. Tradecraft is not a silver bullet, and we all fall short at some time in our careers. But being wrong despite careful attention to the process—for what I call the right reasons—is OK. It's not great but it's OK, if the analysis is transparent, defensible, and repeatable and analysts are able to walk their audience through their reasoning. These challenges are what make the process so important. The tradecraft is a sort of shield, not from being wrong but from wrong thinking and from skipping steps.

Stick to the script: resist "making a call" inconsistent with the evidence. It feels great until you lean over the cliff. Trust the process. No shortcuts. If you're tempted to cut corners or guess, find another line of work, because if you bypass the hard work of Intelligent Analysis, you will make mistakes, some of them costly and indefensible.

Dissents Open New Perspectives, Add Credibility to Assessments, Strengthen Teams

Disruptive behaviors are process wreckers, not dissents. In Intelligent Analysis dissents are as carefully managed as any other phase of the analytic process. Disagreements over KAC ratings are frequent and expected within and among the US intelligence services. Just as explained in chapter 9, at their roots are differences over the validity of the underlying assumptions that support the inference: what caveat (likely/unlikely, highly likely/unlikely…), best characterizes the relationship between the facts and what can be inferred from the facts. Sometimes the disagreements are so deep that they have to be expressed in the form of dissents. But they are data driven--opinions don't count. A clear delineation of differences is important information for the audience. Dissents vary in length but more typically expressed in relatively short paragraphs as statements that read something like this:

- Team members A and B disagree that the reporting is insuffi-
  cient to support the assessment at the expressed level of certainty for the following reasons.... The reasons are evidence
  based.

Intelligent Analysis recognizes that such evidence-based dissents are one
of the process' most important strengths. Encouraging differences and re-
cording them as dissents, and the rationale behind them, is essential to the
transparency that bolsters the credibility of the team's assessment when it's
presented to decision-makers.

The collaborative environment which SATs are intended to foster allows
for disagreements that can be expressed as dissents. Indeed, the more an assessment shifts rightward toward uncertainty on the spectrum where information is thin and estimating probability becomes more difficult, the more
important that dialog and debate become to a team's success.

In Global's case, when an important disagreement surfaced the facilitator
reminded the team that recognizing dissent and integrating it into the assessment is a strength. In Global's case, the engineer and another team member
wanted the building's condition to be the sole linchpin assumption because
not enough was known about it and underestimating would have a cascading
affect across all the other key assumptions. After some discussion, the team
was not willing to jettison economic forecasts but agreed to highlight the dissent in a separate box and make sure that it was part of the final report and
team briefing. Senior management welcomed the differing views. So, while
the team retained the two linchpins the CRO and the board set aside more
funding for deeper inspections and told the sellers they wanted at least $25
million set aside in escrow to fund any unexpected repairs.

The Formal Dissent

The engineer and one other team member familiar with fa-
cility management assess that the condition of the building
should be the sole linchpin assessment. While we agree that
the economic forecast is important, unforeseen problems in
the building could on its own impact all the other assumptions
because of the costs involved and the length of time it will take

Continued on next page

---

to inspect and remedy shortcomings. In our experience across multiple similar buildings cost overruns running in the millions of dollars are common and almost always unplanned in budgets. To start, for example, the engineering report did not include any assessment of space to run new cables and wiring for computer systems and a larger workforce or placement of a cafeteria. In one instance just the cost of running new cables and wiring sent costs well over the estimate and the fixes still did not meet the company's requirements.

This was an important disagreement that provided a different perspective and the team handled it well. Burying the dissent would have robbed the CRO and board of important insights and projected the illusion of unanimity. It also would have undermined the trust needed to tackle Global's next big challenge and raised the risk of organizational silence. Recall that the analytic process has to be repeatable as well as transparent, and defensible. In addition, pressure on the dissenters to back off to preserve the illusion of a unified position would likely have required the team to insert compromise language that weakened or watered downed language in the B.L.U.F. with almost certain serious consequences for the company.

Exercise for Your Project:
Complete, Refine Your Own Assessment's B.L.U.F.

This exercise leans heavily on work you have already done on your assessment. It starts with a review of that work and moves forward from what is known to the outlook, implications, mitigation strategies, and indicators. With this accomplished, you will return to your B.L.U.F. and refine it based on the individual exercises. Please avoid starting over. Of course, refinements are required, but trust already completed work. In particular, after refining the B.L.U.F., turn to the lead inference and make sure it's aligned with the B.L.U.F. It's easier to track the flow if this is done on your computer. Make sure the parts flow and don't hesitate to make any changes.

Who is your decision maker: who will act on your analysis?

_____

What is their KIQ; why is the decision maker asking the question?

_____

What data do you need to collect and array to answer the question?

_____

Enter your B.L.U.F. into the B.L.U.F. template described in Chapter 4. Review the B.L.U.F. up to "impact so far"; does that segment answer the KIQ? Enter it on the computer.

_____

Enter your revised lead inference; make sure it's structured properly and in-cludes the estimated probability that your event or development will occur.

_____

STOP: Go back and check for alignment and clarity.

Turn now to the KAC template described in Chapter 9. You should be ready to move ahead at this point. If not, stop and work through the areas that are not complete or need more work.

List your assumptions in the KAC.

_____

Complete your KAC ratings.

_____

Review the KAC; make sure you have already determined the linchpin assump-tions, other important vulnerabilities, and where the inference might hold up best. Review the estimated probability one more time.

_____

Now, draft the most likely outcome: What is next? It should be based on the KAC results and your own experience. Use the models in the Global scenario described in chapters 9 and 10.

_____

Add a second sentence that includes a level-of-confidence statement in the reporting.

_____

What are the outlook's implications for your decision maker; why should it matter?

_____

Now turn to the Mitigation and Indicator Framework.

For practice, complete the framework for two of your assumptions: the linchpin and one that looks safe. Make sure they align with the KAC.

Linchpin Assumptions (Plus 1, if needed)	1. Why Vulnerable	2. Mitigation Strategy	3. Specific Indicators We Would See If the Mitigation Strategy Is Working	4. Specific Indicators We Would See If the Mitigation Strategy Is Not Working	5. Comments
Linchpin assumption					
Linchpin assumption					
A third optional assumption					

CHAPTER ELEVEN

A Clear Title, Careful Drafting, and Summary Increase Impact

"The main thing I try to do is write as clearly as I can.
I rewrite a good deal to make it clear."

—E.B. White, author, *Elements of Style*

SUMMARY

Main Points

Misspellings, typos, skipped words, and poor grammar raise concerns that other elements of the assessment are also done carelessly. The Four Sweeps breaks down the reviewing process into steps because looking at all four elements at once is difficult. Here is a short summary of the steps:

First Sweep: What is the intelligence message?

- Should answer the KIQ in the title, lead inference and the completed B.L.U.F.

Second Sweep: Structure

- Text should be aligned internally with the B.L.U.F.

Third Sweep: Visuals

- Analytic points, graphics, tables and charts should be clear at first glance and consistent with the text.

Fourth Sweep: Editing Prose

- The prose should be clear, concise, precise, and expressed in the active voice; the grammar should also be correct.

- Reviewing pages laid out horizontally across a table instead of flipping pages helps spot alignment issues and inconsistent or poorly written lead sentences. Reading just the lead sentences of section subtitles should tell a story.

A good summary can determine impact, because a busy reader may have only seconds (literally) to decide to read beyond the title.

- The summary's rule of thumb: any assessment over two pages requires a summary.

- The format is no more than three ticks (bullets) that capture the B.L.U.F. A prose paragraph is unlikely to be read.

Exercises include examples and practice reviewing and crafting a summary and then doing the same for analysts' projects.

CHAPTER 11:
A Clear Title, Careful Drafting, and Summary Increase Impact

"The main thing I try to do is write as clearly as I can. I rewrite a good deal to make it clear."

—E.B. White, author, *Elements of Style*

"Good writing should be transparent, like a windowpane."

—George Orwell, *Why I Write*

Goal: To understand that a "well-packaged" assessment which includes a clear title, short summary, and careful drafting increases its credibility, and that skipping over this step can raise questions about the credibility of the analysis.

Objectives

At the end of this chapter, you will be able to:

- Craft a title that conveys the message in the inference in 8–10 words.

- Apply the Four Sweeps technique to review drafts.

- Draft a summary of longer assessments that answer the KIQ.

- Explain two techniques for self-reviewing assessments. (Chapter is drawn from Cariens, 2012; James, 2009.)

Titles Are a Contract with the Audience

Titles matter. The title is a promise that accurately summarizes the facts and inference in a highly condensed format. Look at the title used in the Global team's completed B.L.U.F.: Charlotte's Growth Forecasts, Building's Condition are Biggest Risks to Purchase. Then look at the lead inference and note how closely they are aligned. There is no difference in tone or message.

- Titles are the entry point to your Intelligent Analysis and a busy audience will likely decide whether to read it or not based on what the title tells them, even if they asked for assessment.

- Titles are analytic, not descriptive. In fact, a strong title combined with a strong lead inference and B.L.U.F. and a good graphic that reinforces the message is a powerful combination that conveys and increases the title's impact.

The list of unhelpful, if cute, titles out there in magazines, journals, and yes, even newspapers is almost endless. *The Economist*, for example, prides itself on clever titles that rarely capture the story line. The addition of subtitles below the puns helps, but then they don't align with the title. So, let's get right to the point: Cute titles are banned from Intelligent Analysis. Don't use them, ever. Meeting all these standards, good titles:

- Alert your reader about a story at a glance.

- Answer the audience's question.

- Capture B.L.U.F. elements, including the judgment's level of certainty, in 8–10 words.

- Avoid sensationalism or hype that can mislead readers.

- Avoid puns and attempts at humor.

The two titles below are examples that fall short of the criteria, in my view, and I am a faithful reader—it drives me crazy. I have lifted them from The Economist (March 16, 2019) which is a consistent—indeed, proud—perpetrator of unhelpful, pun-filled titles. We offer the following (less humorous) alternatives that convey a simpler, clearer message:

- "The Aircraft Industry, Plane Truths: The crash of Ethiopian airlines ET302 shows why a golden age for the world's aircraft may be over" (22 words)

  - Our revision: The Aircraft Industry: ET302 Crash May Weaken Boeing, Airbus Monopolies (10 words)

- "Mental Health, Shrinks, Expanded, There Are Not Enough Psychiatrists. Trained laypeople can often help" (14 words)

  - Our revision: Mental Health: Solving Psychiatrist Shortage May Include Trained Laypeople (9 words)

Below is an example of how an analytic title can evolve from a descriptive title:

1. "Ford's New Engine: Technical Overview" (descriptive)

2. "Ford's New Turbo Engine Unveiled" (reportorial)

3. "Ford's New Turbo Engine Shows Improved Mileage" (This works.)

4. Performance, Mileage-Conscious Buyers Give Turbos High Marks" (This one with a marketing focus works, too.)

Looking at examples 3 and 4, however, how would you expect to see the leads differ? Right, they would likely reflect different levels of estimated probability because example 3 is based on quantitative data and example 4, on qualitative reporting.

EXERCISE:
Craft a Title for Your Own Assessment

Instructions:

Go back to your B.L.U.F. and craft a title that captures its message in under 10 words. This is more challenging than it might seem, because of word limits that force analysts to really think about their message.

Your title: _____

Review it against the criteria. Then add the title first to the template and again to the paragraph as lifted from the template. Read the title and paragraph to make sure all three elements (title, inference, and B.L.U.F.) send a consistent message.

Review Your Text in Four Sweeps

The Four Sweeps review breaks down into four parts the process of reviewing the draft you have worked or stared at for hours. It grew out of analyst training in the late 1980s, and analysts have used the process for decades to facilitate the process of checking text for avoidable errors, especially when self-reviewing. Such proofing matters because, regardless of how well your assessment is thought out and written, decision makers will see mistakes in grammar and spelling as signals that other elements of the assessment are also likely to be flawed.

The Four Sweeps approach is based on the well-founded principle that there are four essential elements to good writing, and they cannot all be reviewed and edited at the same time. The Four Sweeps process helps you and any reviewers focus on each dimension of the assessment separately. It takes discipline to break out the elements and review them four times, especially after you have looked at your work so many times, but it's your responsibility— everything that leaves your hands has to merit an A.

Here are the four sweeps:

First Sweep: Message is Clear and Up Front

- Evident in the title and lead inference.

- Explains the un-obvious to a generalist.

- Expresses confidence level if appropriate.

- Consistent throughout the assessment (ALIGNMENT!).

- Evidence is credible and cited accurately.

- Answers the decision maker's question.

Second Sweep: Structure Provides Product's "Connective Tissue"

- Each section and paragraph advances the story.

- Text is aligned internally with the B.L.U.F.

- Information related to each theme and topic is grouped to-gether.

- Topic sentences capture single main point

- Analytic subtitles tell readers what is ahead.

Third Sweep: Visuals Reinforce Analytic Message

- The analytic point is clear at first glance.

- The message is consistent with the text.

- The visual complements the text (adds detail, explains a point).

- Introductory note ties it to the text.

Fourth Sweep: Error Free Enhances Credibility

- Prose is clear, concise, precise, and expressed in active voice.

- Grammar is correct.

- Text is free of spelling errors, typos, dropped text….

One more helpful hint: Review the assessment using the Four Sweeps and lay the pages out across a table rather than flipping the pages. This approach—even it's just two pages lying next to each other—offers a different perspective. I have found it easier this way to check the overall flow—does the structure make sense; does content align; do the section subtitle and topic sentences flow from the title, lead inference, and B.L.U.F.?

And one more step: ask someone willing to provide honest feedback to read it as well.

EXERCISE:
Review Your Assessment in Four Sweeps

This will be an opportunity to practice the review techniques. It's a two-part exercise. Begin by printing out your analysis, which will facilitate reviewing your assessment.

Instructions:
   First step:

- Undertake the Four Sweeps review. Be ruthless and force yourself to review the four dimensions separately.

- Then lay the pages out on a table as another check on the flow and internal alignment.

- Create another digital copy of the assessment and enter the changes using Track Changes.

   Second step:

Ask a peer you can trust to undertake the same reviews. Buy them lunch or trade roles.

Summary Can Determine Impact

Rule of thumb: any assessment over two pages requires a summary because it may well be the only part read after the title.

In Intelligent Analysis, summaries convey the B.L.U.F.'s key message in three bullets (or ticks) of no more than 8–10 words per bullet. Using the bullet/tick format makes the summary easier to read and understand more quickly than a standard prose paragraph.

EXERCISE:
Craft a Summary

To start, review the sample summary that follows the Global team's revised B.L.U.F. repeated below.

Now return to your now completed B.L.U.F. and craft a summary comprised of no more than three points. Imagine your audience just reading the title and the summary. Will they get your message?

Title	Charlotte's Growth Forecasts, Building's Condition Are Biggest Risks to Purchase
Inference summarizes the B.L.U.F..	Based on a range of reporting and Global's expertise the acquisition team assesses that purchasing the Acme Building is highly likely to benefit Global, provided that important vulnerabilities related to the city's economic forecast and the building's condition are mitigated; other areas of concern are more manageable. We have high confidence in our assessment because independent economic consultants raised questions about the forecast and the initial engineering report pointed to the potential for unseen problems.
What's the new de-velopment?	At the request of the CEO and CRO the acquisition team revisited its initial assessment of the Acme Building's viability as a first purchase in the Charlotte area.
Why now?	Specifically, the CRO wanted to the team to stress test its optimistic assessment using structured analytic tech-niques.
How does it work?	Using SATs and a skilled facilitator to manage the process the team restarted the process that reveals important new insights into the potential benefits and risks related to the purchase.
What's ahead ("so what")?	The team assesses that Global's best course for now is to slow down the acquisition process until the team can probe more deeply into these vulnerabilities.
What are the implica-tions (the "so what of the so what")?	Slowing the process might well cost Global the opportuni-ty to purchase the Acme Building, but Global has been in this situation before and still moved forward at great cost to the company.
What steps can be taken to mitigate risks and exploit and opportunities?	the team is in the process of developing mitigation strate-gies to deal with both the most important vulnerabilities, as well as lesser risks that can rise in importance later in the process.

Here is a sample summary that captures the key points. This is just one approach and the key points can be altered to meet the different needs of stakeholders.

Charlotte's Growth Forecasts, Building's Condition Are Biggest Risks to Purchase

- Drawing on a range of reliable data and diverse expertise, the team's exercise determined that the move to Charlotte would likely benefit Global, but there are risks that need to be managed to protect the company's interests.

- The most important vulnerabilities are limited insight into the area's long-term economic health and incomplete engineering studies of the building that might have overlooked systemic problems.

- We recommend slowing down the acquisition process until mitigation strategies are put in place and progress and indicators are developed to track their effectiveness.

Now, turn to your own assessment and craft a summary for your assessment.

- Title: _____

- Bullet one: _____

- Bullet two: _____

- Bullet three: _____

EPILOGUE

**Our Last Words About You
and Intelligent Analysis**

Certainty	Risk	Uncertainty

Let's close out the book where we started, by reflecting on the certainty-uncertainty spectrum.

Intelligent Analysis's tools and processes are intended to warn organizations when uncertainty begins to replace manageable risk. The higher the uncertainty, the more important Intelligent Analysis becomes. Assumptions—conditions that must hold in order to bring about a good outcome—multiply and become less manageable; reliable data is thin. Opinion and the loudest voices fill in the gaps. Still, pressure for a decision mounts and uncertainty turns decision makers into fortune tellers. The cliff grows closer, but avoiding the fall becomes more difficult.

For senior audiences, whose responsibilities only allow time to review the summaries, Steve and I want to emphasize the importance of assigning skilled analysts and support staff to work through and apply the book's lessons to their assessments. This effort will improve the quality, timeliness, and impact of their work. It's the only way to consistently answer that nagging question: "What am I missing." You will have a shared vocabulary and an understanding of what the analysts have learned and what to expect from their work. They will be well equipped to watch for, and assess, potential threats, and bring a potent set of values about how to do the work that will serve your organization well.

For analysts, Steve and I ask that you think about Intelligent Analysis as a road map or field-tested tool kit that provides a practical approach to decision stress testing. It tests the soundness of high-stakes decisions when the pressures of time, biases, and emotions are most likely to overtake objectivity. Most importantly, we want you to take away a thorough understanding of how, under these circumstances, even the most capable decision makers can consciously or unconsciously leave the world of manageable risk and enter the far less stable and far more unpredictable world of uncertainty where, in the absence of reliable information and experience, opportunities for failure quickly multiply.

Regardless of whether you have devoted time to working through each of the chapters, skimmed them, or read only the summaries and moved on, we promise that organizations that use the tools and processes presented in this book will never think the same way again about how they make their most critical decisions. Intelligent Analysis will always be embedded in the organization's collective brain neurons, reminding each one (a) to slow down before coming to closure and (b) to think more deliberately about what problem the audience is trying to solve and the importance of clearly stating and validating assumptions that underpin assessments.

To close, what you as analysts say can either matters or not.

- Recognize that you are in a position of high trust; it must be earned, and it is easily lost.

- Objectivity is non-negotiable.

- Stay relentlessly focused on your audience; know what they need and when to support decision-making.

- Getting the question right is a collaborative process; do not assume you know what your audience wants to know.

- Continually test assumptions and change the estimated level of probability as new information comes in.

Here is our most important admonition one more time: *trust the process. Always.* And just when you think you are done—that you have the analysis right and the B.L.U.F. clearly written—know that you are not. You can always sharpen the message, update the analysis, review the text for consistency. You are never done. Use the tools that you've practiced in this book.

- Be deliberate and conscious.

- Know the desired outcome.

- Be collaborative; listen first; the answer is always in the room.

- Build expertise; be the decision makers' eyes and ears; warn and point out opportunities.

- Remember that opinions don't count; everything you say or write is evidence based.

- Be clear about what is known and what can be inferred from what is known.

- Have fun; enjoy the challenge. Not every day will be magical, but the work can be rewarding in many ways.

One last time: don't skip steps. Intelligent Analysis is an end-to-end process. It's just too dangerous to cut corners. Jumping to the answer by selecting information to give the audience what they want to hear is at best misleading and at worst poses serious risks to your organization's success. If you are tempted in this direction, think long and hard about finding another line of work.

Appendices

A.   Glossary of Key Terms

B.   Bibliography

C.   Build Your Own B.L.U.F.: A Blank Template

D.   Key Assumption Rating Descriptions

E.   Case Study by Jay Grusin and Steve Lindo: "Target Canada—
A Bad Case of Intelligence Risk Mis-Management"

APPENDIX A:

Glossary

Definitions are drawn from multiple sources and the author's experience. Feel free to disagree.

Actionable intelligence: term used to describe targeted assessments that executive decision makers can act on to meet known requirements; applies to both private and public sector decision makers.

Analytic tradecraft: also known as tradecraft, a term used to describe a set of standardized tools and processes that analysts in the US intelligence services have used for decades to produce consistently objective, evidence-based assessments for a wide range of audiences.

Assessment: conclusion based on underlying Intelligence information, analysis, and assumptions.

Assumption: as used in intelligence analysis, a condition that must persist to support an estimate of probability that an event or development will occur at the assessed level of likelihood that is subject to change with new information.

Assumptions, working: first draft of conditions that must persist to support an estimate of probability; can number up to as many as 10 or 15 assumptions.

Assumptions, key: also called drivers or variables. A list of no more than six assumptions drawn from the list of working assumptions considered to be the most important that must persist to support the estimate of probability. The limit is six because these conditions must persist; dozens don't have to persist.

Assumptions, linchpin: the one or two key assumptions determined to be the most critical to supporting the estimate of probability; subject to change (more or less certain) with new information. Use of the term in the US intelligence services gained currency in the mid-1990s as a way of focusing analysts' assumptions on what mattered most in shaping the most likely outcome.

Big data analytics: also called predictive analytics. Computer-assisted process of collecting, organizing, and analyzing large sets of data to discover patterns and other useful information.

Bottom Line on the Bottom: term that describes a written assessment where the main point or message does not become apparent until the end of the piece; most common in academic papers and journals.

Bottom Line Up Front: in Intelligent Analysis and across the US intelligence services and military, a tightly formatted lead paragraph that provides audiences with actionable intelligence in a complete response to specific audience questions. Each sentence provides a key element of the response, which includes an assessment of the event, the most likely outcome, and why it matters to the audience.

Cognitive biases: according to Richards Heuer in *Psychology of Intelligence Analysis*, "mental errors caused by our simplified information processing strategies. . . Cognitive bias does not result from any emotional or intellectual predisposition toward a certain judgment, but rather from subconscious mental procedures for processing information. A cognitive bias is a mental error that is consistent and predictable."

Debiasing: term used to describe the reduction of bias, particularly with respect to objective Intelligent Analysis. Structured Analytic Techniques (see below) are a suite of tools intended to mitigate the impact of biases in the analytic process.

Data-driven analysis: term used in this book to describe the process of analyzing qualitative or quantitative information to look for trends, patterns, or relationships not readily apparent to decision makers. Transforms data into intelligence.

Estimating the level of probability: the process of determining the likelihood that an event or development will occur, which is described using a set of agreed-upon vocabulary.

Forecast vs. prediction: in this book, the terms are used to distinguish between developing the most likely outcome that is anchored in reporting as opposed to just looking ahead and essentially guessing.

Inference: a conclusion based on facts as known. In this book inferences are structured as A + B →C. *A* and *B* are facts as known and *C* is the implied inference or insight/conclusion that can be drawn. The arrow (→) is a stand-in for the expressed estimate of probability that C will occur (*likely, unlikely,* etc.) expressed using an agreed-upon vocabulary.

Indicators: also known as signposts or indicators of success or change. In Intelligent Analysis, developed to track the impact of mitigation strategies on the validity of key assumptions that support the most likely outcome. Based on reporting they must be observable, metrics-based, and readily accessible to the audience.

Intelligence Community Assessment (ICA): The Office of the Director of National Intelligence (ODNI)'s premier publication. It is an assessment that is agreed upon by all the US intelligence services.

Intelligence Community Directive (ICD): established by the Director of National Intelligence as the principal means by which the ODNI provides guidance, policy, and direction to the intelligence community. ICDs that set analytic standards are an example.

Intelligence failure: defined by the CIA's Center for the Study of Intelligence as a systemic organizational surprise resulting from incorrect, missing, discarded, or inadequate hypotheses.

Internal alignment: term used to describe the consistency of the message throughout an intelligence assessment; that is, the audience sees the same bottom line whether expressed in the title, lead inference, Bottom Line Up Front section, or the outlook. *See probability drift.*

Intelligence cycle: term used to describe the steps in the production of Intelligent Analysis, which is produced and displayed as a never-ending circle: requirements collection, processing, analysis and production, and dissemination, then back to requirements again.

Intelligent Analysis vs. Intelligence Analysis: For the purposes of this book, they overlap completely in terms of tools and processes, but use of the term Intelligent Analysis is intended to signal utility well beyond their traditional role in the US intelligence services.

Key Assumptions Check (KAC): a framework that is part of the suite of Structured Analytic Techniques intended to test the validity of the assumptions and confidence in the reporting underpinning the inference and their potential impact on the estimate of probability of the inference.

Key Intelligence Question: question developed collaboratively between analysts and the audience that answers a specific question; it's crafted against a set of criteria and answered in the Bottom Line Up Front.

Level of confidence (LOC): a formal assessment of the quality of the sources measured separately from the level of certainty in the reporting.

Office of the Director of National Intelligence (ODNI, or DNI): The Director of National Intelligence serves as the head of the intelligence community, overseeing and directing the implementation of the National Intelligence Program budget and serving as the principal advisor to the President, the National Security Council, and the Homeland Security Council for intelligence matters.

Organizational silence: occurs when participants in a discussion choose to remain on the sidelines rather than risk criticism or retaliation for speaking out.

Practical drift: a concept developed by Scott Snook and defined as the slow uncoupling of practice from written procedures.

Premortem: part of the suite of Structured Analytic Techniques that, unlike a postmortem, assumes the bad outcome and looks for systemic points of vulnerability.

Probability: the likelihood that an event or development will occur expressed in an agreed-upon vocabulary.

Probability drift: term used extensively in probability theory. In intelligence analysis it is the absence of internal alignment; that is, it refers to a shift in the estimated level of probability within the same intelligence assessment.

Quantitative data: information or data based on quantities obtained using a quantifiable measurement process.

Qualitative data: in contrast, information that records qualities that are descriptive, subjective, or difficult to measure.

Senior or executive decision maker: the intended recipient of actionable intelligence.

Structured Analytic Techniques (SATs): a suite of qualitative frameworks that rely on structured discussions to help analysts mitigate the adverse impact on objective analysis of their cognitive limitations—biases, emotions, and mindsets that work against objective analysis.

US intelligence services: collective term used in this book to describe the US Intelligence Community, a group of 18 separate United States Government intelligence agencies and subordinate organizations that work separately and together to conduct intelligence activities to support the foreign policy and national security of the United States. The Office of the Director of National Intelligence (ODNI) plays a coordinating role over the US Intelligence Community and leads the presidential briefing team.

APPENDIX B:

Bibliography

Armstrong, Fulton T. 2007. "Ways to Make Analysis Relevant but Not Prescriptive." Center for the Study of Intelligence.

Cariens, David. 2012. *Intelligence and Crime Analysis: Critical Thinking Through Writing*. Shiplake House Publishing.

Center for the Study of Intelligence. 2007. "Words of Estimative Probability." Studies in Intelligence.

Davenport, Thomas. 2013. "Big Data and the Role of Intuition." *Harvard Business Review*.

Davis, Jack. 1997. *A Compendium of Analytic Tradecraft Notes*, vol. 1, notes 1–10. CIA Directorate of Intelligence.

Fishbein, Warren, and Gregory Treverton. 2004. "Rethinking 'Alternative Analysis' to address Transnational Threats." *Kent Center Occasional Papers* 3(2).

Gartin, Joseph. 2019. "The Future of Intelligence," Studies in Intelligence 63(2).

Grusin, Jay, and Steve Lindo. 2018. "Target Canada—A Bad Case of Intelligence Risk Mis-Management." Intelligent Risk Management LLC.

Heuer, Richards J., Jr. 1999. *Psychology of Intelligence Analysis*. Center for the Study of Intelligence, Central Intelligence Agency.

Kahneman, Daniel. 2014. "Premortem to Eliminate Thinking Biases." YouTube video, 3:17. December 29.

Klein, Gary. 2007. "Performing a Project Premortem." *Harvard Business Review*, September.

Major, James S. 2009. *Communicating with Intelligence*. Professional Intelligence Series, no.1. Concept Publishing.

Morrison, Elizabeth Wolfe, and Francis J. Milliken. 2000. "Organizational Silence: A Barrier to Change and Development in a Pluralistic World." *Academy of Management Review* 25(4).

National Intelligence Council. 2012. *Global Water Security*. Intelligence Community Assessment.

National Intelligence Estimate (NIE). 2002. *Iraq's Continuing Programs for Weapons of Mass Destruction*. (Declassified Key Judgments.)

Office of the Director of National Intelligence. 2006. *Intelligence Community Directive 201: National Foreign Intelligence Warning System.*

Office of the Director of National Intelligence. 2015. *Intelligence Community Directive 203: Analytic Standards.*

Office of the Director of National Intelligence. 2016. *Intelligence Community Directive 206: Sourcing Requirements for Disseminated Analytic Products.*

Petersen, Martin. 2011. "What I learned in 40 Years of Doing Intelligence Analysis for US Foreign Policymakers." *Studies in Intelligence* 55(1).

Pfeffer, Jeffrey, and Robert Sutton. 2006. "Evidence-Based Management." *Harvard Business Review*.

Ramsey, Diane M., and Mark S. Boerner. 1995. "A Study in Indications Methodology." Center for the Studies of Intelligence.

Sinclair, Robert. 2010. "Thinking and Writing: Cognitive Science and Intelligence Analysis." Center for the Study of Intelligence. (Originally published in January 1984.)

Snook, Scott, 2000. Friendly Fire: The Accidental Shootdown of U.S. Black Hawks over Northern Iraq

Taleb, Nassim N. 2008a. Interview with Constantine Sandis. *Philosophy Now*.

Taleb, Nassim N. 2008b. "The Fourth Quadrant: A Map of The Limits of Statistics." *The Edge*, September 15.

US Government. 2009. *A Tradecraft Primer: Structured Analytic Techniques for Improving Intelligence Analysis.*

US Intelligence Services. "Quality Framework." This is a composite from several examples.

Walton, Tim. *Consumer Knowledge, Collaboration Shape Key Intelligence* Question, undated

Walton, Tim. Intelligence Question Framework Embodying Standards: in a Textbook, Sherman Kent School for Intelligence Analysis at CIA."— Presentation transcript, undated

APPENDIX C:

Build Your B.L.U.F.:
Moving Your Assessment Forward

The final exercise pulls together all the work done so far on the project. In one exercise all the connective tissue in the intelligent analytic process is visible to be refined and reviewed again . . . and again against all the lessons learned in the book.

You have already done the hard thinking, so use your work sheets but know that when your analysis is done, drafting the assessment should be straight-forward and comparatively easy.

- Use the B.L.U.F template below.

	TITLE
Inference summarizes the B.L.U.F.	
What?	
Why now?	
How does it work?	
What's the impact so far?	
What's ahead ("so what")?	
What are the implications (the "so what of the so what")?	
What can be done to mitigate risks and ex-ploit opportunities?	

Remember that when you think that you are done, you are not. It can always be better, sharper, more useful to the audience.

What is your working title?

What is your key judgment (in the form of an inference)? For example, reporting over the last two months indicates . . . suggesting (making it likely, probably, etc.).

_____
_____
_____
_____

Who is/are the specific audience(s) for your assessment?

_____
_____
_____
_____

What is the purpose of your assessment for this/these audience(s)? (inform, warn, target, allocate resources)

_____
_____
_____

What is your Key Intelligence Question?

_____
_____
_____

What data did/will you collect to answer the question?

_____
_____
_____

How do you plan to array the data?

_____
_____
_____

Now answer the question with the Bottom Line Up Front.

Below is the B.L.U.F. template. Answer in full sentences. Break out each sentence and label it.

What is the development that made you write? (Recent reporting indicates ... suggesting/pointing to a new trend, pattern, relationship ...)

_____

_____

_____

Why are you writing now? (This matters now because ..)

_____

_____

_____

How does it work? (Important but optional: is there process or the way a crime unfolds that decision makers need to know about to understand the piece?)

_____

_____

What has been the impact of the development so far? (What does the data show? It may be that there is not information that points to any impact at this point.)

_____

_____

_____

List the Assumptions that Underpin Your Lead Inference

1. Write out each assumption that underpins the inference: What conditions must persist to maintain the validity of my most likely outcome?	2. How strongly does the evidence support the inference's estimated probability? (1-10)	3. What is the level of confidence in the evidence? (1-10)	4. Would this assumption's failure cause any others to fail? (1-10)	5. What is the impact on the inference's estimated probability if the assumption does not hold? (1-10)
One too many				

What is the most likely outcome? (Use the results of the Key Assumptions Check.)

_____

_____

_____

What are the implications of the most likely outcome for your decision maker?

_____

_____

_____

Complete the Mitigation and Indicator Framework.

Assumptions: should be written in full

1. Mitigation Strategy	2. Specific Indicators We Would See If the Mitigation Strategy Is Working	3. Specific Indicators We Would See If the Mitigation Strategy Is Not Working	4. Comment

What the columns mean:

To start, each assumption is addressed on a separate sheet. The assumption is repeated in full above the matrix. Next, based on the KAC, where does the assumption fall? Is it a linchpin, important vulnerability, or relatively safe assumption?

Column 1: The mitigation strategy. Describe in detail what action needs to be taken.

Column 2: Indicators the strategy is working. Think of it this way: what would we expect to see if the strategy results in a positive change in any of the KAC ratings. The indicators are expressed as metrics.

Column 3: Indicators the strategy is not working. Again, expressed in metrics. These metrics are not just the opposite of those in column 2.

Column 4: Comments. Included here are observations about the strategy or the metrics.

The example in Chapter 10 shows what a completed framework would look like. It uses an assumption that for now is considered safe.

STOP HERE: GO BACK AND ENSURE ALIGNMENT

If You Were to Expand This Lead Paragraph into a Longer Paper

To help keep you focused as you develop the paper, turn each part of the B.L.U.F. into a question to be answered with reporting. Simply list what you would use or where you would look.

To make it easier to draft an analytic topic sentence, just use the elements of the B.L.U.F. in the form of sub-questions that are answered in the lead.

Title

B.L.U.F.: The full paragraph

Topic answers the question: What is the development?

- Supporting data

- Supporting data

- Supporting data

Topic sentence: Why now?

- data

- data

- data

Topic sentence: How is ___ accomplished?

- data

- data

- data

Topic sentence: What is the impact so far?

_____

- data

- data

- data

Topic Sentence: What is the most likely outcome?

_____
_____
_____

- data

- data

- data

And so on . . .

APPENDIX D:

Key Assumptions Rating Descriptions

This table will help you assign ratings to the key assumptions which you identified for your own project in Chapter 9. Long-term, it will serve as a reference tool to help you express the link between the ratings in your Key Assumptions Check and the underlying data, and how to explain these links to your audience. Remember that the ratings are intended to anchor your data-driven discussions, and do not imply precision.:

1. Select the ratings which best represent your assessment of each of the key assumptions in columns 2, 3 and 4

2. Explain to your audience the ratings and their underlying rationale in clear, descriptive language

Remember that the ratings are intended to anchor your data-driven discussions, and do not imply precision.

How to use this table

1. Test your assessment of each of the Key Assumptions against the rating descriptions in columns 2, 3 and 4 and select the rating which best represents your evaluation of the underlying data.

2. In column 5, the table does not offer a set of rating descriptions because, as explained in chapter 8, this is where you indicate which of the key assumptions you consider to be the linchpin(s). Because the set of key assumptions underlying any specific proposition are unique, a common set of impact rating descriptions is not applicable. Instead, select ratings in column 5 which rank order your expectation of each key assumption's potential impact on the inference, based on the available evidence.

3. Finalizing your KAC ratings is an iterative process, which gradually crystallizes you or your team's assessment. No matter how long you deliberate and debate your initial set of ratings, upon review expect to make changes, likely more than once, because your assessments evolve during the rating process.

Write out each assumption that underpins the judgment: *What conditions must persist to maintain the validity of my most likely outcome?*	How strongly does the evidence support the inference's estimated probability? (1-10)	What is the level of confidence in the reliability of the evidence? (1-10)	Would this assumption's failure cause any others to fail? (1-10)	What is the impact on the inference's estimated probability if the assumption doesn't hold? (1-10)
	0 There is no relevant data	0 There is no relevant data or the data sources have no credibility	0 If this assumption fails, none of the other key assumptions will be affected	
	1 There is negligible relevant data			
	2-3 There is some relevant data, but the data is conflicting or incoherent	1 The objectivity and reliability of the data sources are highly questionable	1 If this assumption fails, it's very unlikely that it will cause any of the other assumptions to fail	
		2-3 The objectivity and reliability of the data sources are questionable		
	4-5 There is a significant amount of relevant data, but the data is not complete or consistent		2-3 If this assumption fails, it's unlikely that it will cause any of the other assumptions to fail	
		4-5 The objectivity and reliability of the data sources are unknown		
	6-7 The data is not complete or consistent but it supports the inference's estimated probability		4-5 If this assumption fails, it may or may not cause one or more of the other assumptions to fail	
		6–7 The data sources are known to be reasonably objective and reliable		
	8-9 The data is complete and consistent and supports the inference's estimated probability		6–7 If this assumption fails, it's likely to cause one or more of the other assumptions to fail	
		8-9 The data sources have a strong track record of objectivity and reliability		
	10 The data is complete and consistent and strongly supports the inference's estimated probability	10 The data sources have been verified	8–9 If this assumption fails, it's very likely to cause one or more of the other assumptions to fail	

APPENDIX E:

Target-Canada:
A Bad Case of Intelligence Risk
Mis-Management

Dr. Jay Grusin, The Analytic Edge and Steve Lindo, SRL Advisory Services, 2018 Intelligent Risk Management LLC. (published online)

Every high-stakes business decision is unique, but when it comes to risk analysis, they all share three common challenges—time pressure, infrequent occurrence and an unruly cocktail of facts, data, opinions, and assumptions. Considering these challenges, it's not surprising that the gallery of corporate disasters has many rooms. This article explores one of them. As the reader will discover, it's a story of too much bias and too little discipline. It also provides an exemplary platform for demonstrating the preventive power of Intelligence Risk Management techniques in high-stakes business decisions.

Target Canada—A Self-inflicted Disaster

In its first international venture Target opened some 130 stores in Canada between March and December in March 2013: the last one closed two years later in March 2015. The company's hasty retreat across the border left behind some $7.5 billion in sunk costs and close to 18,000 Canadians lost their jobs. In hindsight business pundits penned numerous articles assessing why Target Canada collapsed so quickly. For the most part they looked back and blamed the readily apparent failure of the IT systems and logistics. Customer service, culture, and other business school platitudes made the lists. Their not surprising assessments promised to fuel "they shoulda known better" case studies for years. More platitudes.

In our view, their collective "schadenfreude" has kept them focused on the symptoms, not the causes of a much deeper problem that destroyed Target Canada. At its root we assert that it was an intelligence failure, for which we have coined the term "intelligence risk." This type of risk occurs when information overload, inconclusive data, cognitive biases, different perspectives, organizational influence, and intense time pressure all lead to catastrophically short-sighted and/or imprudent decisions. We argue here that the venture was doomed from its inception in 2011, when the then-CEO made a hasty and ill-considered purchase of some 200 leases from collapsing Canadian retailer Zellers.

The operation was vast in scope. In order to make our case we looked at the whole history of avoidably bad decisions and decided to focus most intently on what reportedly occurred at the last senior review meeting held in mid-February 2013.[i] At that meeting, the CEO of Target Canada, Tony Fisher,

---

[i] For the account of that mid-February meeting we relied heavily on: Joe Castaldo, *Disaster: The Last Days of Target [Canada]*, Canadian Business, January 2016.

gave the go-ahead to launch in three weeks despite clear warning signs that it would collapse.

In our look-back at Target's Canadian fiasco we want to make three key points:

- First, Target's failures were above-all process failures: the mechanics of how the senior team made tactical and strategic decisions were deeply flawed, which is all too common across organizations. None of the assumptions they made heading into the opening held up. None.

- Second, we contend that private sector decision makers and intelligence analysts share the same world of risk, uncertainty, and biases. The same structured analytic techniques (SATs) which US Government intelligence analysts have used for decades to bring additional rigor and discipline to their analysis are equally suited to identifying and managing intelligence risk in the private sector, lowering the incidence and severity of error. [ii]

- Third, SATs are qualitative tools, built around structured discussions. They are not replacements for how decisions are made, whether based on "gut feelings" or predictive analytics. Rather, our contention is that, regardless of how you get to the decision point, you need to stop and check your assumptions.

In a high-stakes situation, such as the Target Canadian fiasco, what all the stakeholders need to know is critically important, and what needs to be known by others cannot be buried in noise and rancor so that it's unable to surface. When decision meetings unravel, even well-understood problems remain unresolved, risks only grow, and the business's environment becomes more and more toxic. This is what happened to Target. Emotions and deeply rooted biases replaced evidence-based decision making.

This dimension—the failure of process—is what the pundits missed.

[ii] The best assessment of the challenges of being an analyst is Richards J. Heuer, *Psychology of Intelligence Analysis,* Center for the Study of Intelligence, Central Intelligence Agency, 2009. Hereafter referred to as "Heuer."

A look back at Target Canada's light-speed rise and collapse through the eyes of an experienced intelligence analyst and a financial risk expert shows how using SATs at key decision points during the planning process would have helped Target's senior managers to stand back and, drawing on readily available expertise, make an honest assessment of the intelligence risk they faced.

Cognitive Biases: A Common Trap

The literature on biases is vast, but here we want to focus on the extent to which cognitive biases or how what goes on in our heads shapes how we process information[iii]. Once cognitive biases take hold they are difficult to overcome; we become hard wired and resistant to change. Accounts of what happened at Target's February meeting indicate that at that moment Tony Fisher's cognitive biases and those of the broader Target management team put the entire enterprise at risk. Consciously or not, they interpreted unfolding events as they wanted to see them despite overwhelming contrary evidence. The reporting indicates that they believed deeply and without reservation that Target's corporate culture of success could overcome any challenge.

Fisher, a 38-year-old wunderkind, did not so much ignore the bad news as filter the information through his lens of Target's deeply embedded culture of success. This culture had fueled Fisher's cognitive biases. Overweening self-confidence in his own capabilities and his company's impeccable track record erased memories of two years of bad decisions. Fisher did not believe he could lose until he did and led the company over a cliff—and he lost his job and took the CEO with him.

US Government Intelligence analysts have long integrated structured analytic techniques into their analysis to help mitigate the weight of cognitive biases of the kind that trapped Fisher. Analysts live in a world of ambiguity and uncertainty where the risks of failure in making daily high-risk judgments can translate into much more severe consequences for failure than the collapse of a department store chain. Their smaller margin for error means simply arriving at a consensus is not good enough: the judgments must be right all the time. The assessment of Iraq's weapons of mass destruction program and ISIS' rapid break through are just two well-known examples of what can happen when judgments are insufficiently challenged.

[iii] Heuer, pp. 111-113

The intelligence community has identified multiple cognitive biases that that can infect decision-making.[iv] Figure 1 shows the biases judged most common among intelligence analysts. Biases from each quadrant were readily apparent in Fisher's decision-making as well (in italics).

Perceptual Biases	Biases in Evaluating Evidence
Expectations. *We tend to perceive what we expect to perceive.* **Resistance.** *Perceptions resist change even in the face of new evidence.* **Ambiguities.** *Initial exposure to ambiguous or blurred stimuli interferes with accurate perception, even after more and better information becomes available.*	**Consistency.** Conclusions from a small body of consistent data engender more confidence than those drawn from a larger body of less consistent data. **Missing Information.** It is difficult to judge the potential impact of missing evidence, even if the information gap is known. **Discredited Evidence.** *Even evidence proven wrong may not be sufficient to change perceptions quickly.*
Biases in Estimating Probabilities	**Biases in Perceiving Causality**
Availability. Probability estimates are influenced by how easily we can imagine or recall similar instances. **Anchoring**. *Probability estimates are adjusted only incrementally.* **Overconfidence**. *In determining levels of certainty, we are often overconfident, especially experts.*	**Rationality**. Randomness, accident, and error tend to be rejected as explanations for observed events. **Attribution**. *Behavior of others is attributed to some fixed nature of the person or country, while our own behavior is attributed to the situation in which we find ourselves.*

Figure 1: Common biases that can impact decision-makingiv

The risk these biases pose to decision-making underscore the value structured analytic techniques can bring to the process, especially when teams sort through contradictory information and sharp differences spark emotions that can interfere with a tight focus on the data. In fact, in the early 2000s in the wake of investigations that followed the September 2001 attacks Congress mandated their use by intelligence analysts and they remain an integral part

---

[iv] A Tradecraft Primer: Structured Analytic Techniques for Improving Intelligence Analysis, Tradecraft Review, Volume 2, Number 2., page 2. This source is the best guide to structured analytic techniques.

of ongoing analytic training. To varying degrees, they are used routinely by a significant percentage of intelligence community analysts, especially those working on high-risk, high-demand accounts.

- Analysts have found that they can shape meeting agendas, help integrate the equities of multiple players from different components and leverage expertise and disciplines that bring different perspectives to the table.

- In addition, analysts often explain in their finished products and briefings how they used SATs to convey how they reached their judgments.

The Key Assumptions Check: A Window into Target's Collapse

Analysts have developed well over 20 SATs. Most are qualitative, using frameworks that shape conversations and drive a team toward a judgment; some more complex tools have started to use off-the-shelf software programs. We have opted for the former, drawing on two well-tested and extensively used diagnostic techniques to show how SATs might have steered Target Canada away from disaster: The Key Assumptions Check (KAC) and Indicators/Signposts of Change (Indicators).

- *The KAC* measures the validity of assumptions that underpin judgments, including the level of certainty and confidence in the information and their interdependence.

- *Indicators of change* are used to track events to see if the judgment continues to hold up as new information becomes available.

The KAC is especially well suited to review where the Target leadership derailed. In his article, Castaldo used the team's decision-making at the February meeting as the jumping off point to provide context for readers on the decisions that preceded that gathering.

Using the data and comments he gathered from dozens of interviews with employees, we can approximate the decision-making dynamics sufficiently to show how the KAC could have brought more rigor and discipline to the discussion, and perhaps saved Target Canada and made Fisher a hero instead of unemployed.

Before we go any further, it's important to clarify what we mean by assumptions.

Definitions of assumption abound, but for intelligence analysts and our analysis of Target, **assumptions are defined as conditions that must persist for a judgment to remain valid at the stated level of certainty** (*probably, likely, unlikely, almost certainly, remotely, could, might, would*).

Example: Commuter calls home: "I am on the road now. Traffic looks good so I will be home in 30 minutes."

Multiple assumptions underpin the judgment's high level of certainty. The validity of this judgment is based on the evidence that supports the commuter's assumptions; in this case his judgment holds if traffic continues to look good. If new information (accident ahead, boulder falls in the road, RV's blocking left lane) then the judgment's level of certainty changes as well. The commuter will arrive home, but the time becomes uncertain and so does the judgment ("will be home" becomes: "I am not sure").

Because of the importance of assumptions in decision-making, they need to be clearly stated, understood by everyone, and tested against new information. Unstated assumptions are just that: conditions that for some unexplainable reason you are certain will persist, but it is not clear to anyone else why. The key assumptions check forces you to articulate and test them

---

Figure 2: Common Understanding of Assumptions

Testing the KAC at Work: The King of Troy Forecasts the Battle's Outcome

A rendering of the well-known legend of Helen of Troy illustrates how the KAC can check your assessments. You know the story: to retrieve Helen, the Greeks launch a thousand ships. The Trojan King is brimming with confidence. The people are worried, but without any basis beyond his "gut feeling," the King tells his people not to worry:

> "Troy is well prepared for the siege; we are well supplied, and our walls have never been breached, so the Greeks will be kept on the beach."

The army chief is not so sure and wants his intelligence analysts to test the unconscious (read: unexamined) assumptions that the King deeply believes are true. He does not want to tell truth to power without an updated assessment. The validity of the King's judgment will hinge on research (or intelligence gathering) that tells the army chief whether the Greeks have/have not improved their capabilities sufficiently to threaten Troy. Once the team of analysts have reported back, the King's assumptions are then retested using the **KAC**. The judgment may stand as stated or be expressed with less certainty (probably, likely, about even, unlikely or highly unlikely), in which case the King will have to move quickly to make any adjustments if he is to keep the Greeks on the beach and come clean with his subjects.

So, what story does the **KAC** tell? The Trojan analysts have been hard at work and they deliver the completed **KAC** (Figure 3). The analysts' assessment is based on a series of structured conversations moving from left to right on the matrix that test the judgments from multiple perspectives.

1) Write Out Each Assumption That Underpins the Judgment: What conditions must persist to maintain the validity of my most likely outcome?	2) Level of Certainty in Evidence (1-10)	3) Level of Confidence in Evidence (1-10)	4) Would this Assumption's Failure Cause Any Others to Fail (1-10)	5) Impact on Judgment if Assumption Does Not Hold (1-10)
1) Greeks Intend to Fight	6	3	6	6
2) Greek Weaponry Remains the Same	4	8	8	9
3) Trojan Internal/ External Intelligence Remains Accurate	5	6	10	10
4) Supplies Remain Sufficient	7	8	5	3
5) Trojans Remain Loyal	9	9	10	10
(6-N) One Too Many				

Figure 3: Can the Greeks Be Kept on the Beach?

What Each Column Tells You:

Column 1: *Lists the key assumptions:* From a broad list of 20 or so, the team of analysts selects the most important: *these are the ones which must remain true for the judgment to remain valid at the King's level of certainty.* They are written out in full sentences. This grid allows the team to list only five key assumptions. The number is intentionally restricted because the more assumptions listed as key, the more variables must be controlled to support the key judgment, which raises the risk that the judgment will not hold.

Column 2: The group assigns each assumption a strength of evidence rating, based on a review of the reporting views of the evidence supporting the assumption.

Column 3: Assesses the confidence the group has in the reliability of the sources of all the reporting. For example, how reliable are the Trojan spies; any surprises?

Column 4: Measures complexity—the interdependence of the judgments. Can the assumption stand if another is shown invalid? *Which assumption is most likely/least likely to create a cascading effect?*

Column 5: Rates the expected impact on the judgment. *It is not a result of the averaging of the numbers, but a separate discussion that could require adjustments elsewhere.*

In each instance, structured discussions—not personalities—among stakeholders drive the process. Once completed, the team will see patterns emerging that can point to areas of the judgment's strengths and vulnerabilities. In turn, these drive the forecast of the level of risk and decisions on next steps.

As Figure 3 shows, the analysts agree that the King's confidence is dangerously misplaced. The one piece of good news is assumption five: The King can count on the Trojans' loyalty; the other assumptions vary in certainty.

- The most critical assumptions are two and three, but they are also the ones that the army chief is least certain will hold because of the lack of good reporting. These become what analysts call the "linchpin" assumptions. They are the most critical vulnerabilities, and the Trojans were least certain about them. The assessment got his attention.

- With that in mind, the army chief explains the city's key vulnerabilities and steps that can be taken to shore up their intelligence. This assessment would likely include Greek trickery and novel weaponry, such as gift horses.

The King decides to come clean with his subjects and says problems have surfaced, and we have a plan to deal with them in the next few days.

Back to Target: Chronology of a Failure

The timeline below is a composite of several different chronologies that appeared in the press and business journals tracking the growing public face of Target Canada. Invisible to the public ahead of the opening was the massive infrastructure construction to support the scores of stores to be opened simultaneously. Most critical among the hundreds of other daily decisions were completing the three massive distribution centers, installation of the complex IT systems that drove the logistics system, and the hiring and training of up to 20,000 new employees.

January 2011: Target takes aim at Canada: CEO Steinhafel announces the purchase of 220 leasehold interests from Zellers, Inc for $1.8 billion and announces that Target will invest over $1 billion more in store upgrades before opening 100-150 stores in 2013. Target names Tony Fisher, a 38-year-old highflyer who was Vice President of merchandise operations, to be CEO of its Canadian business.

May 2011: From the 220 leases, Target picks an initial 105 as store locations across all 10 Canadian provinces. Another 18 are to open by mid-year.

August 2011: Hiring begins of what should be between 18,000 and 20,000 employees.

February 2012: Fashion designer Jason Wu is brought in to whet Canadian appetites for Target Chic.

August 2012: The Canadian public's ire is raised after Target officials imply that former Zellers customers are not their target demographic.

Mid-February 2013: Senior management has its last pre-launch meeting and decides Target is ready to break into the Canadian market.

March-December 2013: 124 stores open—120 of them before July. Goal met: Target leaders ecstatic.

April 2013: Shoppers flock to Target's Canadian stores and already see empty shelves and limited stock

August 2013: Only 27 percent of shoppers surveyed say they are "very satisfied with their shopping experience."

September 2013: Sales hit $275 million, but losses reach $169 million.

December 2013: 70 million Target customers are hit by the second largest credit card security breach in US history

February 2014: Losses now total close to $1 billion in the first 11 months.

May 2014: Target Canada CEO Tony Fisher is fired. Mark Schindele replaces Fisher; first quarter losses total $211 million.

July 2014: Brian Cornell is named Target Corp. CEO; focuses on Canadian stores as losses continue to mount.

November 2014: Cornell sounds warning to market analysts.

January-March 2015: Cornell announces plans to close Canadian stores in mid-January. Last store closes in March. Target stock bumps up four percent. Wall Street lauds Cornell for pulling the plug and turning the company's focus back to the US.

Failure: Target Never had a Chance

Castaldo's article remains the best account of the collapse. Looking back, he argues that the project was in trouble the minute Target bought the leases in a hasty and ill-considered purchase. The company greatly overpaid for the leases ($1.8 million), because the CEO was concerned that Wal-Mart would make the buy first and he believed that the best chance to break into the crowded bigbox market—and start to recoup costs—was to jump in on a large scale rather than piecemeal. The CEO had spent his entire highly successful career with Target and led the company to expansion and steady revenue growth; he was confident in the company's well-validated culture of success. According to Castaldo's interviews, Target personnel attributed the CEO's confidence that his decision was sound in his belief that his two underlying assumptions would hold:

- Target was capable of launching a massive opening within two years starting from zero.

- This could be achieved because the Target model was readily transferable outside the US.

The CEO's wildly optimistic deadline and assessment of the start-up's complexity shocked the staff. Both the CEO's critical assumptions were quickly disproven.

- A close read of Castaldo's article indicates that, in fact, these two assumptions rapidly morphed into over a dozen as the project's complexity became more apparent and dependencies multiplied. Fisher's overconfidence in Target's corporate culture and the power of the brand that drove his process never faltered.

- The account suggests the team at least questioned these assumptions at different points in the process, but the problems that surfaced on opening day indicate they were not properly, if ever, addressed.

To give you a sense of the depth of Target's real vulnerabilities, we constructed a list of assumptions that at least two senior team members mentioned to Castaldo or to another journalist or that another observer pointed out. None held up. None. In no particular order:

- Zellers locations are good enough: Target is a destination.

- A website can come later.

- The stores will "feel" like Targets.

- Target can double Zeller's sales.

- The stores will be profitable in year one.

- Three new distribution centers will be ready.

- The logistics system will keep all planned 133 stores stocked.

- Target's US-based IT system would be able to "talk" to the IT systems chosen for Target Canada—SAP, JDA, and Retalix—in 18 months.

- Problems with IT systems can be fixed while stores are operating.

- Inventory data processing can be outsourced to India.

- Staff and managers will be ready without standard extensive training.

- Price differences with US stores won't matter.

- Target's long and successful "can-do" culture will triumph.

The three distribution centers opened but because of the decision to out-source inventory data processing to India they were not properly integrated into the logistics system. So, they only belatedly functioned properly when it was too late to matter.

As the problems mounted, the company deployed more resources to Canada, eventually growing to some 400 staff and managers in the days ahead of the opening. Even so, a sense of doom steadily overtook the staff. Castaldo's account indicates that daily planning meetings had become increasingly tense and the CEO less visible. Fisher, however, clung to his belief that he could push the team to solve the deepening problems. Asking for a delay would have been a sign of weakness, he reasoned. Clearly, he was aware of the challenges, but the CEO's assessments of the intelligence risk and the scope of Target's vulnerabilities became subjective and way more optimistic than the data warranted.

Multiple biases, long baked into the Target culture, worked against any other outcome from the moment the company bought the empty stores in 2011. Together, these biases created an echo chamber that just repeated company mantras and management glossed over even the most critical—and readily apparent—vulnerabilities.

The February 2013 meeting was the last chance to stop the launch. According to Castaldo's interviews with senior officers, a group of them gathered one last time to assess the company's readiness to launch in less than a month. According to the reporting, one of the three team members in charge to the IT systems warned Fisher that unresolved supply chain problems threatened to wreak havoc with customers. The other officers reportedly remained silent hoping Fisher got the message; he did not and decided to launch.

An Imagined KAC Exercise Unpacks Fisher's Calculus

Let's conduct another key assumption check, this time imagining how Fisher might have assessed the soundness of his decision to launch ahead of that meeting. Most importantly, Castaldo's account suggests Fisher judged that integration of the multiple software packages could be performed while the stores were operating. He also reasoned that:

- Delays would impact new hires and compound mounting financial pressures.

■   Target's long-standing and deeply embedded culture of success would be able to overcome any problem and his senior
staff would not fail.

Based on Castaldo's interviews (no comment from Fisher) the figure (Figure 4) below represents our reconstruction of Fisher's risk assessment.

1) The condi-tions that must persist for the judgment to remain valid	2) Strength of Evidence Supporting Assumption (1-10 highest)	3) Level of Con-fidence in the Reporting (1-10 highest)	4) Impact on Other Assump-tions if It Fails (1-10 highest)	5) Impact on Key Judgment if Assumption Does Not Hold (1-10 highest)
Target Brand Will Bring Shoppers to Zeller Sites	10	10	THE	ONLY
Distro System Operational	10	10	ASSUMPTIONS	TARGET'S
Staff Meets Target Criteria	10	10	WILL	CAN DO CULTURE
IT Systems Operational	10	10	ALL	MATTERS (REALLY)
Corp Culture Trumps All	10	10	REMAIN VALID	10
Eight More Assumptions	10	10	NO PROBLEM	10

Figure 4: Our reconstruction of Fisher's risk assessment

Though exaggerated for effect, our imagined KAC tells a clear story: he
was supremely confident that managers raised in Target's strong corporate
culture would find a way around the long list of problems without asking for a
delay. Target Canada paid a high price for his errors in judgment.

Let's briefly assess each of the key assumptions against the expertise that
Fisher's staff reportedly had at hand but ignored. Note the assumptions' close
interdependence. The **KAC** would have captured that cascading effect.

Assumption 1: The Target brand alone will bring shoppers to even out-of-the way Zeller sites.

- For the first time, Target stores were integrated into strip malls versus traditional and easily recognizable stand-alone buildings.

- Target calculated that its brand would draw shoppers, even to marginal neighborhoods that did not map to Target's US-based demographic.

- Ahead of the launch, well-established rivals Costco and Wal-Mart took important steps to prepare for the new competition. Dozens of other mid-sized businesses also upped their game.

Assumption 2: The three distribution centers will be operational.

- The three centers were constructed and stocked.

- Their ability to stock the stores spread across the country, however, depended on functioning logistics systems which in large part had been outsourced to India.

- When inventory backed up, Target was forced to store the overflow in dozens of rented storage facilities.

Assumption 3: The staff, including managers, will be "Target-ready."

- Target managers were generally hired right out of college and put through extensive training to absorb the company's unique culture. Employees also received ongoing training specific to their departments, much of it from their experienced managers.

- Target Canada employees and managers received training, but it was not of the same depth.

- One more point: Target promised that it would retain as many of Zeller's former employees as possible, which proved to be untrue: the chain drew only one to two percent of the nearly 20,000 new hires from laid-off Zellers workers. Reports tell of deep resentment in affected communities.

Assumption 4: The new IT systems would be operational.

The CEO believed the IT systems developed by Target in the US would easily transition to the new environment, but the technicians quickly learned that could not work in French or in Canadian currency.

- To address the problem Target turned to System Applications Product, known widely as SAP, to install an enterprise-wide system only 18 months before launch. This system works well, but it is complex, requires extensive staff training, and experts agree that it needs years for retailers to fit their workflows into the software—not the other way around.

- To fix that problem Target Canada decided to introduce two new software products along with SAP: JDA's supply chain management software and Retalix, which is omnichannel software, to establish an interface with their existing US-based system.

- As we already noted, Target also decided to outsource inventory data entry to a company in India. Quality control was weak, mistakes mounted and the entire inventory control system—the secret to Target's success—collapsed.

- Consequently, warehouse managers did not know what to ship and so guessed, which left Target's shelves sometimes full of laundry detergent but devoid of what shoppers really wanted. Pictures of empty shelves or aisles of laundry soap, long lines at registers, and pictures of sloppy displays quickly appeared in the Canadian newspapers.

- Also, because the IT systems were not in place and operational when the stores opened, the undertrained staff did not understand the point of sale or stock control systems.

- Fisher believed the systems could be fixed while the stores were in operation.

Assumption 5: Target's can-do culture would overcome these challenges.

- The chain did make important fixes heading into 2014, but by then customers had fled the stores.

- Protestors appeared asking Zellers to come back. Customers felt betrayed. The chain's death spiral was terminal.

An Evidence-Based Risk Assessment

Below is an alternative reconstructed version of Fisher's **KAC** that integrates this more sober assessment of his assumptions. This time, it's the product of his team working alone and presenting him with their independent findings (see Figure 5).

What conditions that must persist for the judgment to remain valid	2) Strength of Evidence Supporting Assumption (1-10 highest)	3) Level of Confidence in the Reporting (1-10 highest)	4) Impact on Other Assumptions if It Fails (1-10 highest)	5) Impact on Key Judgment if Assumption Does Not Hold (1-10 highest)
Target Brand Will Bring Shoppers to Zeller Sites	4	8	8	7
Distro System Operational	5	9	10	10
Staff Meets Target Criteria	4	8	7	8
IT Systems Operational	4	10	10	10
Corp Culture Trumps All	4	10	10	10
Eight More Assumptions	5	10	10	10

Figure 5: The experts' assessment of the timing of the launch

The results of the expert-facilitated **KAC** exercise tell a very different story.

■   Not surprisingly, the exercise confirmed that the readiness of the IT systems and confidence in Target's corporate culture were the two most critical assumptions. They were also the most vulnerable to failure and were critical to the validity of the other assumptions. The findings warranted a warning to delay the launch.

■   To reach that assessment, the team agreed that the evidence supporting the assumptions was weak (column 3), and they had high confidence that this was the case (column 4). So, they were most certain that this was the most critical vulnerability.

■   The company's vaunted corporate culture, for example, had never been tested outside the US, and the IT experts knew that the IT infrastructure was months away from being operational.

■   Beyond these linchpin assumptions, other parts of the system also showed serious weaknesses and needed to be addressed.

Hindsight: KAC Outcome Drives Mitigation Strategies and Indicators

The results of the alternative **KAC** would have turned the team toward mitigation strategies. The problems that surfaced in the exercise told the team that fixes were required end-to-end, but some were more important than others. There was no mystery about what they had to do. The team also knew that their strategies had to be tested extensively before the launch and then repeated periodically to look at problems as they surfaced or resurfaced. Their goal would have been manageable risk.

■   As part of the process, the team would have developed a set of indicators to track progress against a new set of metrics. Indicators would be observable events that were diagnostic: observable and collectible. These indicators could also be used to track events, spot new trends, and warn of change.

- Suitable indicators might have included: training completed, successful tests of the IT systems, or results from store openings.

In this scenario, Fisher would have traveled to Minneapolis with his team and used their **KAC** to make the case for a delay. Headquarters would have listened, and five months later Target Canada's stores would have opened to stay.

Final Take Away: SATs are About Managing Risk, Not Avoiding It

Intelligence analysts and private sector decision makers share a world of intelligence risk and uncertainty awash with information of uncertain reliability. SATs are tools proven capable of helping navigate risk, to more effectively and efficiently identify it and develop mitigation strategies. They are not about avoiding risk but bringing rigor and discipline to identifying it. So, there are good reasons why intelligence analysts and private sector counterparts should use the same tools that they have used for decades to test their judgments and leverage expertise and diverse views. Even in the most intense environments these can bring more rigor to how decisions are made, methodically focusing on the data, and minimizing the impact of emotions and personal differences.

Could SATs have made a difference to Target? Frankly, a company with Target's track record should have been able to manage without them. Target's leaders had control over all the variables. All of them. Then why and how did a world class brand bungle an opportunity to break into an important market? In retrospect, Target Canada's leadership underestimated the risk and uncertainties of moving into a foreign market (yes, Canada is a foreign country), and they had no real idea what they were in for. The decision to put a 38-year-old merchandise manager in charge and the chaos that dominated the development process from start to finish makes that point. Under these conditions SATs could well have at least forced the conversations that needed to take place to stop the list of key assumptions growing from two to over a dozen. Target should have known better.

About the Authors
Jay Grusin is a former CIA Senior Officer He has an MA and a PhD from The University of Arizona.

Steve Lindo is a risk manager with over 20 years' experience in the financial and nonfinancial sectors. He is an instructor and course designer for Columbia University's MS in Enterprise Risk Management.

Made in the USA
Coppell, TX
05 August 2021

59995807R00154